Fine WoodWorking

Best Workshops

From the **Editors of** *Fine Woodworking*

The Taunton Press

The Taunton Press
Inspiration for hands-on living®

THE TAUNTON PRESS, INC.
63 South Main Street, PO Box 5506
Newtown, CT 06470-5506
e-mail: tp@taunton.com

EDITOR: Christina Glennon
COPY EDITOR: Marc Sichel
INDEXER: Jay Kreider
COVER & INTERIOR DESIGN: Carol Singer
LAYOUT: Cathy Cassidy

Fine Woodworking® is a trademark of The Taunton Press, Inc.,
registered in the U.S. Patent and Trademark Office

The following names/manufacturers appearing in *Fine Woodworking Best Workshops* are trademarks: 3M™, Band-Aid®, BlastBuster™, Bosch Airsweep™, Coban™, DAMPLOCK®, DRYLOK®, Ecogate®, Elvex®, ESS®Ice 2.4™, FastCap®, Gore® CleanStream®, Grizzly Industrial® Inc., HardiePlank®, Hocks Noise Brakers®, Krazy® Glue, Kreg®, Lie-Nielsen Toolworks®, Lithonia Lighting®, Moldex®, National Electrical Code®, Oneida®, Paslode®, Plexiglas®, Plugmold®, Rockler Woodworking and Hardware®, SketchUp®, Steri-Strip™, Tegaderm™, Trend®Airshield®, Veritas®, Visual™, Wiley X™, Wilson®, Woodcraft®, X-Acto®.

LIBRARY OF CONGRESS CATALOGING-IN-PUBLICATION DATA IN PROGRESS

ISBN 978-1-62113-009-3

PRINTED IN THE UNITED STATES OF AMERICA
10 9 8 7 6 5 4 3 2 1

This book is complied from articles that originally appeared in *Fine Woodworking* magazine. Unless otherwise noted, costs listed were current at the time the articles first appeared.

ABOUT YOUR SAFETY: Working wood is inherently dangerous. Using hand or power tools improperly or ignoring safety practices can lead to permanent injury or even death. Don't try to perform operations you learn about here (or elsewhere) unless you're certain they are safe for you. If something about an operation doesn't feel right, don't do it. Look for another way. We want you to enjoy the craft, so please keep safety foremost in your mind whenever you're in the shop.

ACKNOWLEDGMENTS

Special thanks to the authors, editors, art directors, copy editors, and other staff members of *Fine Woodworking* who contributed to the development of the chapters in this book.

Contents

Introduction

When it comes to woodworking, people get caught up in gearing up. And that's understandable, since the right tools often spell the difference between fun and frustration. But the space you work in is just as important. Are you warm enough there? Can you see well enough to do your best work? Is it a jumble of loose lumber, tools, cords, and sawdust, or is it clean and organized, with everything at your fingertips and nothing underfoot? Do you have a rock-solid workbench with good vises, ready for fine handwork?

If the answer to any of these questions is no, you are probably experiencing some level of frustration every time you go out, or down, to the shop. You might even hesitate to go in the first place.

That's why you need this special compilation from the pages of *Fine Woodworking*. Drawn mostly from the magazine's most popular issue, the *Tools & Shops* annual, these articles cover every aspect of a comfortable and hard-working space, whether you are starting from scratch or upgrading the shop you have.

Leaving no stone unturned, *Fine Woodworking Best Workshops* starts with the overall structure and layout, and then covers your best options for climate control, lights, wiring, dust collection, workbenches, cabinets, lumber racks, and much more. And we don't forget the basement woodworker either, with a special chapter on working down under.

Start upgrading your shop today, and you'll be surprised at how much fun woodworking becomes.

—Asa Christiana
Editor, *Fine Woodworking*

Best Tips for Basement Workshops

THOMAS McKENNA

I n medieval times, miscreants and criminals were tossed into the bowels of a dungeon for their offenses. Below ground, these dungeons were dark, dank, foreboding places, characterized for centuries as hideous homes for torture or cramped imprisonment.

It may be a stretch to compare a basement shop to a dungeon, but they do have similarities. Like a dungeon, a basement is a hole in the ground and attracts all manner of moisture, with issues such as mildew, rust, even small floods. Basements aren't flooded with natural sunlight either; single incandescent fixtures are the norm, usually scattered where you don't need them. On top of that, basements are where household items go to die, so space is tight.

Still, for lack of an alternative, many woodworkers set up shop in the basement and have to deal with any or all of these medieval horrors. To help them out, we asked our extensive and experienced online audience for tips on making a basement workshop drier, brighter, and more space-efficient. We also asked folks how they prevent noise and dust from infiltrating the living areas above.

The response was overwhelming, and we got plenty of nifty solutions to common problems. We used those ideas to create a virtual basement shop that is as comfortable to work in as it is unobtrusive to the rest of the household.

The ideal basement shop

On www.FineWoodworking.com, we asked our enthusiastic audience how they avoid the common pitfalls of a basement shop, such as too little space and light and too much moisture, dust, and noise. With their input, we created this virtual basement shop that tackles every issue.

LOCK OUT MOISTURE

Water is the enemy of all things wood and metal, causing unsuitable moisture levels and rusting valuable equipment. It also leads to mildew and mold growth. To reduce moisture problems, direct water away from the foundation and seal the interior with a moisture-blocking paint. It also helps to run a dehumidifier.

LET THERE BE LIGHT—AND LOTS OF IT

Add enough fluorescent fixtures to illuminate the space uniformly. Use task lights in storage areas or on tall machines, such as a bandsaw, to supplement the overall lighting scheme.

USE NOOKS AND CRANNIES FOR STORAGE

Basement shops often compete for space with family needs (laundry areas and playrooms) and utilities (water heaters and furnaces). So you must take advantage of every storage opportunity. You can hang racks and cabinets on stud walls built along the perimeter. Though not aesthetically pleasing, pegboard is a convenient place for tools, clamps, and jigs. Also, take advantage of oddly shaped areas, storing lumber and offcuts under stairs or in other tight spaces.

DO NOT DISTURB THE HOUSEHOLD

Let's face it, building furniture is a noisy hobby, and when you're engaging your passion below the rest of your family, the muffled roar can be annoying. We got some great tips from readers on how they manage sound transmission, ranging from isolating framing from drywall, to beefing up the basement door, to muffling shop vacuums and compressors, to simply not working after hours.

DON'T CHOKE ON DUST

There's not a lot of airflow in a basement, so airborne dust will just hang in the air or migrate to living areas above. To control and capture it, use a dust collector and install an air cleaner. To prevent dust from tracking upstairs on the bottom of your shoes, place a doormat at the bottom of the stairs or wear shop shoes.

Defend against wetness.
To reduce moisture levels in the shop, coat the walls and floor with a moisture-sealing paint, such as DRYLOK, and add a dehumidifier.

How to keep moisture at bay

Basement walls are concrete, a porous material that allows moisture penetration if you don't take measures to stop that migration. It's well worth the effort, though. Here in the Northeast, for instance, many basements are moist, and folks who have basements are familiar with the term "musty." In summer, there's an odor in the basement that's impossible to miss but hard to pinpoint. In winter, the cold, moist air can chill even your fingernails. And the moisture does not just create an uncomfortable working environment. It also will rust your tools and increase the moisture content of lumber to undesirable levels.

If you get standing water regularly, you may have issues that need to be addressed by a professional waterproofing contractor before placing expensive tools and materials in harm's way. But if you simply have a damp space, there are many ways to fight the fog.

Look outside—If you're battling moisture, the cause may be rooted outside the house.

Check that the house gutters are not clogged and that the downspouts are directed away from the foundation. Where possible, try to grade the property so that it slopes away from the house. This may be easier said than done.

Get a dehumidifier—One of the first things we heard from our online responders was to add a dehumidifier. You can get one at any home center. When you install the dehumidifier, make a habit of emptying it regularly, especially during the humid summer months.

Seal walls and floor—You can reduce moisture by sealing the walls and floor with a moisture-blocking paint, such as DRYLOK® or DAMPLOCK®. These thick coatings have the added benefit of giving the area a bright face-lift that reflects light.

Guard against rust—Finally, you can fight rust directly by placing desiccants in tool drawers or coating surfaces lightly with paste wax (rubbing waxed paper on machine tabletops works).

Fight dust and noise migration

Dust is a known carcinogen, so it's important to prevent as much of it as possible from floating around. If you work in a basement, the dust also becomes a nuisance upstairs, as it will migrate into living areas. So get a dust collector and an air cleaner to help keep the particles at bay. You'll also appreciate the fact that there will be less to sweep up.

Along with dust, a woodworker's passion for building things comes with another inhospitable by-product: noise. When you're working below the living area of your home, you must be mindful of others above. Our online survey uncovered some nuggets that help reduce the noise that can invade living areas.

Keep compressor to a low hum

Compressors and shop vacuums are not friendly to your ears, so enclosing them in a cabinet will help muffle their ugly decibel levels. When enclosing a compressor, be sure to allow for air circulation by adding vent holes. The same idea can also be used to silence a shop vacuum.

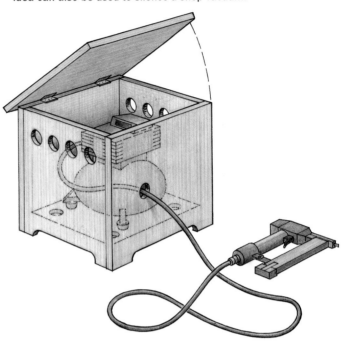

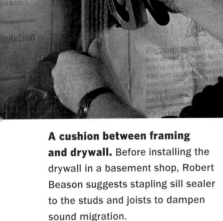

A cushion between framing and drywall. Before installing the drywall in a basement shop, Robert Beason suggests stapling sill sealer to the studs and joists to dampen sound migration.

Separate drywall from framing— One way to reduce sound transmission is to isolate the drywall from the framing. You can install resilient metal channel (www.truesoundcontrol.com) in the ceiling, but a cheaper alternative is stapling polystyrene sill sealer (available at home centers) to studs and ceiling joists to create a cushion between the wood and the drywall. Insulation between framing also will help reduce sound transmission; the higher the R-value, the better the insulation will dampen sound.

Put a lid on your compressor and shop vacuum— Although you can't put a muffler on your

Keep dust downstairs. These shoes were made for working. Art Mulder uses a pair of shop shoes and a mat to avoid tracking dust into living areas.

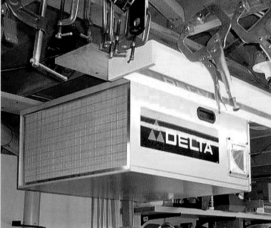

Quiet cleaner. Serge Duclos says he's reduced vibration from his ceiling-mounted air cleaner by separating it from the joists with 6-in.-wide, ¾-in. plywood strips.

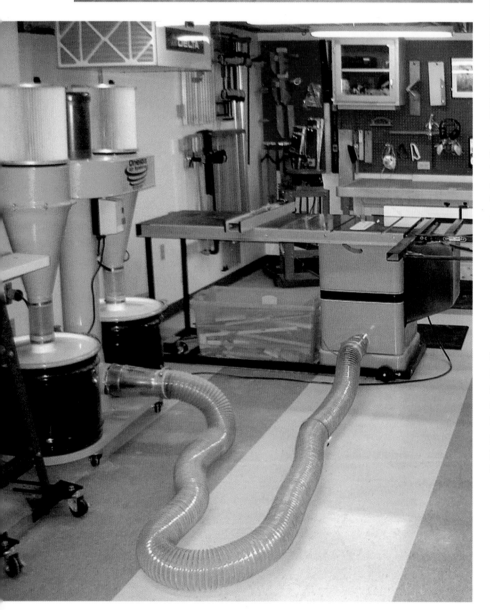

Serious dust collection. Most readers with basement shops agree: A dust collector and an air cleaner are must-haves. Dave Verstraete uses a portable 2.5-hp collector, which provides plenty of capacity in a small footprint.

Brighten the space. For even illumination, Dave Verstraete added banks of fluorescent lights. He also laid down light-colored tiles and painted the walls white to add reflectivity. "When I switch on the lights in my basement shop, it feels like I am outside on a sunny day," he says. Although uniform lighting is the goal, some taller tools, like a bandsaw, cast inconvenient shadows. To eliminate those, use strategically placed task lights (below).

tools, you can reduce the output of two of the more annoying accessories in the shop: the compressor and the shop vacuum. By housing each of these in a soundproof chamber made of plywood and acoustic padding, you drop the noise level of each machine. Just make sure the box has enough holes or vents for airflow.

Get a better door—One of the unique aspects of a basement shop is that there's often a door leading directly to the living areas of the home. Choosing the right door, or modifying your existing one, can help reduce the amount of noise and dust that enters the home. For advice in that area, I turned to veteran *Fine Homebuilding* editor Chuck Miller, who's also a talented woodworker.

High-frequency noises generated by routers and shop vacuums get in through cracks, Miller says, while low-frequency sounds, such as those generated by a deadblow mallet on a workpiece, migrate through mass. Miller recommends treating the basement door as though it were an exterior entry, where you want to stop air infiltration.

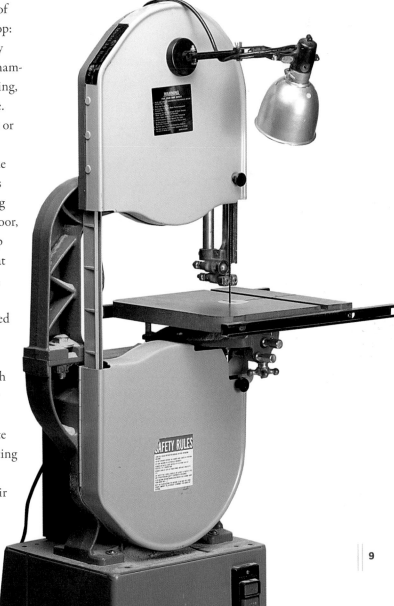

Perfect place for small parts. Chris Walvoord shares a basement with a family playroom and guest bedroom, so his space is ultra-tight. To make the most of it, he built shelves under his stairs to hold offcuts and jigs.

Your first choice is to install a heavy, pre-hung exterior door, with all the attendant weatherstripping in place. The weatherstripping will cut down on the high-frequency sound, and the mass of the door itself will muffle the low-frequency noise. If you don't want to add a new door, retrofit the basement door with weatherstripping along the door stops, and add a vinyl sweep to the door bottom.

Pump up the lighting, and make the most of space

By nature, basements don't get natural light, so you need a boost here. Typically, basement lighting schemes are not well-thought-out by builders. You often get a small handful of single bulbs scattered here and there. But you can change the lighting scheme to create a more inviting, comfortable work area.

The goal is to create uniform lighting from corner to corner, and fluorescent fixtures are the most economical way to do it. If you have existing incandescent fixtures, replace them with banks of fluorescent lights to illuminate as much of the space as possible. If you don't have existing fixtures and wiring, it's worth the investment to hire an electrician to run the wiring and install the fixtures.

To help with light reflectivity, paint the walls white and coat the concrete floor with epoxy paint. Another option is to lay down light-colored vinyl tile. Treating the floor not only helps with light reflection, but it also fights moisture and makes it easier to sweep up any debris.

If you need to, add task lighting at your bench or at machines that cast shadows on their own tables, such as a floor-standing drill press or a bandsaw. It's also beneficial to illuminate storage areas.

As with most woodworking shops, a basement can get filled with equipment quickly. But basement spaces can be small to start with, and often store stuff for everyone in the family, so storage for your lumber, tools, and accessories becomes even more of a challenge.

Many readers suggested using narrow or oddly shaped areas, such as the space under stairs, to store lumber and scraps. Those with larger basements built separate storage rooms around their furnaces and water heaters. This solution not only creates a neat storage option, but it also isolates the utilities from wood dust. Some folks simply store most of their wood outside or in the garage, bringing in stock as they need it.

Don't overlook walls and ceilings. Dave Verstraete hung clamps on the wall (top), and put up pegboard near his workbench for jigs and tool accessories. Serge Duclos hangs longer pipe clamps under the ceiling joists (above), leaving the wall free for other types of clamps.

An alcove for lumber.
This area in Robert Beason's basement is too small to work in, so he converted it to a lumber storage area. A rolling storage cart fits perfectly between the lumber rack and basement wall.

Some readers built wood stud walls over the concrete surfaces, making it easy to hang cabinets, lumber racks, or other storage systems. The bottom line: Use spaces smartly, and you'll stay well organized and avoid mixing your lumber scraps with the laundry.

Working in a basement is not so bad

A basement may not be the ideal place to set up shop, but for many folks it's the best option. Instead of toiling in a dungeon, you can create a clean, well-lighted place. In the end, you'll be more comfortable and so will your housemates—a win-win for everyone.

Turn Your Garage into a Real Workshop

MICHAEL PEKOVICH

I set up shop in the two-car garage of my Connecticut house when I started at *Fine Woodworking* 14 years ago. Coming from California, I wondered why so many folks in this area chose to work in their cramped basements rather than their spacious garages.

But when November came around, I understood. The propane heater I had installed was no match for the uninsulated roof and walls, cold concrete floor, and leaky garage doors. After emptying a 60-gal. propane tank in less than a month, my shop quickly became a three-season workplace and its floor space was increasingly devoted to bikes, camping gear, and chicken feed.

The Big Picture

With its drafty doors and concrete floor, Pekovich's uninsulated shop was limited to warm-weather woodworking. Even in the summer, the low ceiling, dark walls, and minimal lighting made the space feel cramped and dreary. By adding insulation, improving the lighting, and replacing the garage doors with shopmade carriage doors, he transformed the space into a comfortable, year-round workspace.

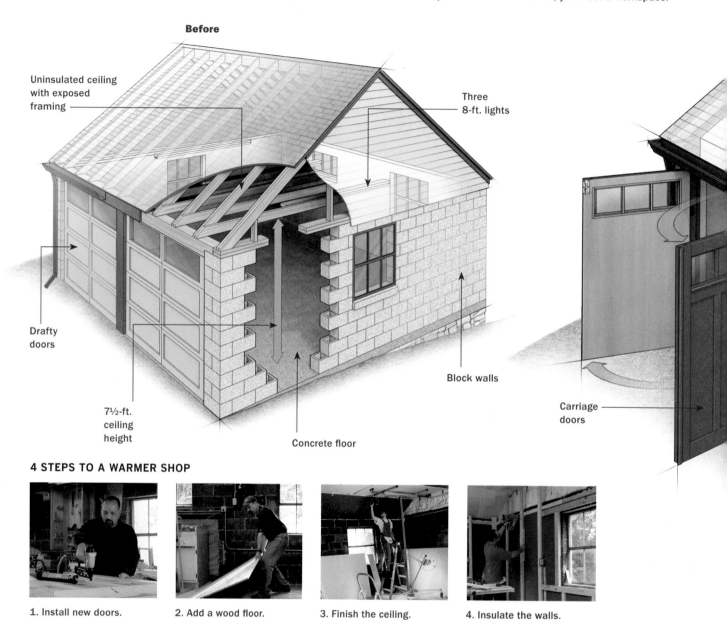

Before

Uninsulated ceiling with exposed framing

Three 8-ft. lights

Drafty doors

7½-ft. ceiling height

Block walls

Concrete floor

Carriage doors

4 STEPS TO A WARMER SHOP

1. Install new doors.

2. Add a wood floor.

3. Finish the ceiling.

4. Insulate the walls.

With access to the *Fine Woodworking* shop at work, I asked myself if I even needed a home shop, but after sharing the shop for years and watching rust develop on my woodworking machines at home, I finally decided I really needed my own heated workspace. This meant insulating the floors, walls, and ceiling; hanging and finishing drywall; and installing new doors. I also bought a manufactured shed to house all of the non-woodworking items that had been slowly encroaching on my workspace.

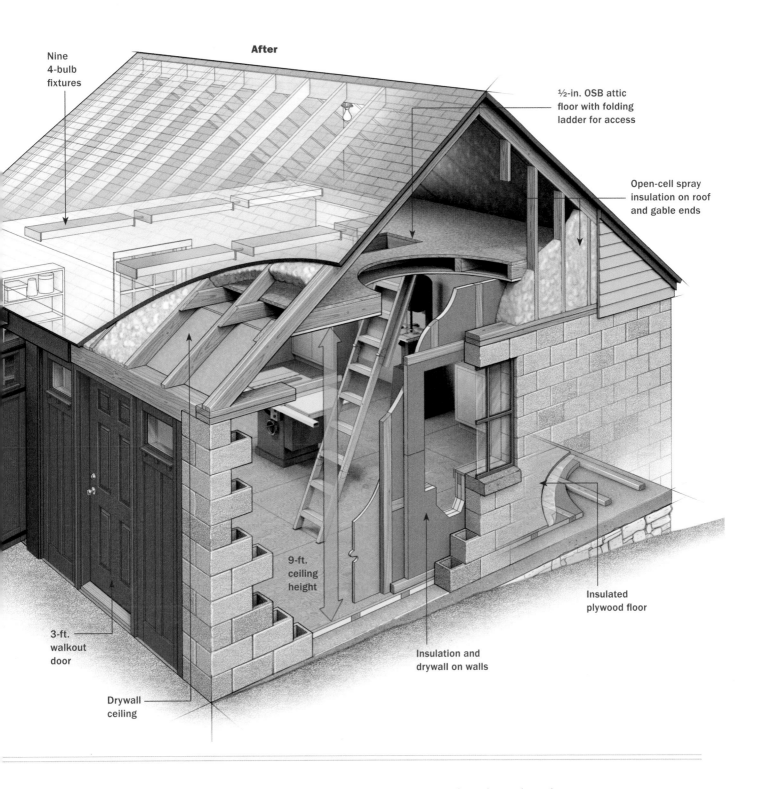

After

Nine
4-bulb
fixtures

½-in. OSB attic
floor with folding
ladder for access

Open-cell spray
insulation on roof
and gable ends

9-ft.
ceiling
height

Insulated
plywood floor

3-ft.
walkout
door

Insulation and
drywall on walls

Drywall
ceiling

I'm a woodworker, not a carpenter, so a lot of the tasks on this project were new to me. Fortunately, with the folks at *Fine Homebuilding* just down the hall, I had access to decades of collective building knowledge. Admittedly, some of the building solutions I came up with might not be realistic on a typical building site where speed and efficiency dictate how to accomplish every task, but they made sense to me as a woodworker on a very tight budget. I hope they make sense to you, too.

Poplar frame, plywood skin. A groove in the center of the 1½-in.-thick poplar stock receives stub tenons formed on the ends of the door rails with a dado set (right). Although most of the strength comes from the plywood skins, stub tenons help keep everything square during the large glue-up (below). Once the glue dries, the interior compartments are filled with 1½-in.-thick rigid insulation.

Pine dresses up the plywood. Pekovich applied flat pine pieces to create a frame-and-panel effect and an Arts and Crafts look.

Two garage doors—two different approaches

It was easy to see I was losing many of my heating dollars through the gaps in the garage doors. Weatherstripping and insulation kits are available for doors in good repair, but my old rotting doors had to go. The question was how to replace them. I thought about a set of steel insulated doors, but I didn't like the idea of hoisting open a roll-up door in the middle of winter and letting the cold air rush in.

Instead, I decided to replace one of the overhead doors with a normal walk-out door (see the drawing on p. 19). This would provide easy entry and create a few extra feet of much-needed wall space. I did this by framing in a pair of narrow panels that would flank an inexpensive, prehung steel entry door.

Each panel consists of a 2x4 frame faced with CDX plywood (rated for exterior use). The frame is filled with rigid insulation and covered with drywall on the interior face. To dress up the exterior, I glued and nailed pine boards to the plywood for a frame-and-panel look. Windows with square corbels below the sill added an Arts and Crafts element that would complement my home's bungalow style.

For the second bay, I needed a different approach. Even though I never intend to park a car in the space, I still wanted to leave a door wide enough to drive through in case we ever decide to sell the house. I also like the idea of having a large opening for machinery and lumber, and letting in sunshine on nice days.

Instead of a roll-up door, I opted for a pair of swing-out carriage doors. I thought the

Two options for drafty garage doors

MAKE LIGHTWEIGHT CARRIAGE DOORS

Filled with rigid insulation and covered with a frame-and-panel treatment, Pekovich's shopmade carriage doors are an attractive and energy-efficient upgrade over conventional overhead garage doors. Torsion-box construction makes them lightweight yet very strong—and simple to build.

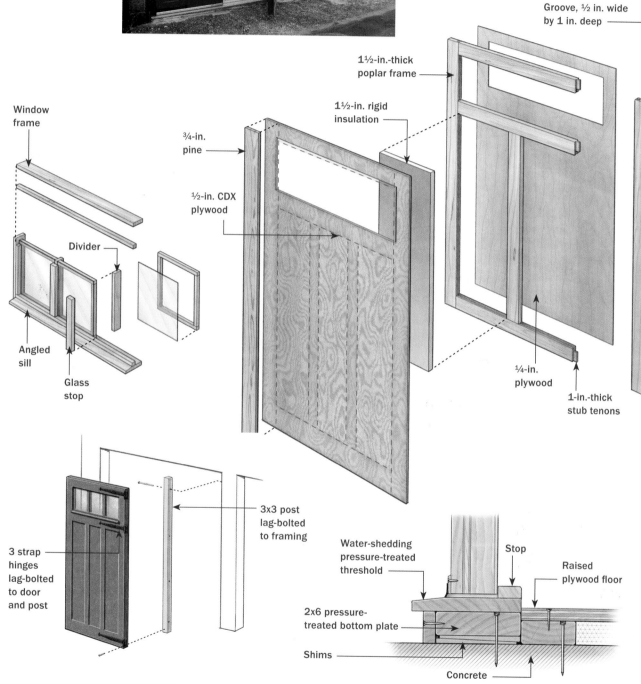

Window frame

Divider

Angled sill

Glass stop

¾-in. pine

½-in. CDX plywood

1½-in. rigid insulation

Groove, ½ in. wide by 1 in. deep

1½-in.-thick poplar frame

¼-in. plywood

1-in.-thick stub tenons

3 strap hinges lag-bolted to door and post

3x3 post lag-bolted to framing

Water-shedding pressure-treated threshold

2x6 pressure-treated bottom plate

Shims

Stop

Raised plywood floor

Concrete

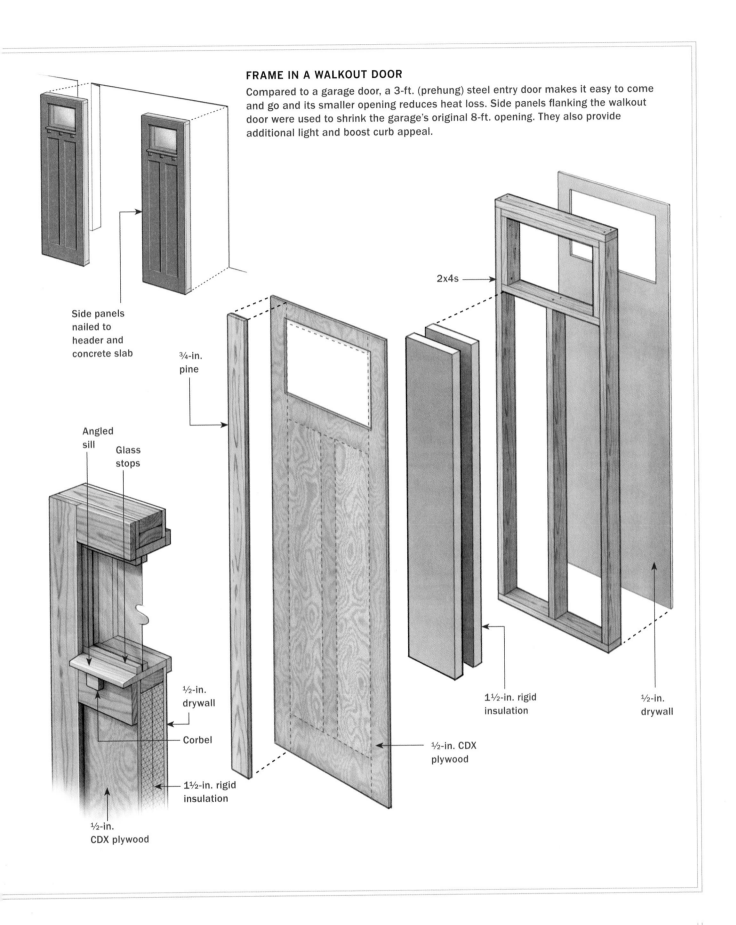

FRAME IN A WALKOUT DOOR

Compared to a garage door, a 3-ft. (prehung) steel entry door makes it easy to come and go and its smaller opening reduces heat loss. Side panels flanking the walkout door were used to shrink the garage's original 8-ft. opening. They also provide additional light and boost curb appeal.

Side panels nailed to header and concrete slab

¾-in. pine

Angled sill

Glass stops

½-in. drywall

Corbel

1½-in. rigid insulation

½-in. CDX plywood

½-in. CDX plywood

2x4s

1½-in. rigid insulation

½-in. drywall

½-in. CDX plywood

carriage doors would be easier to weather-seal and would offer more insulation. Eliminating the garage door's overhead tracks would also give me additional headroom and provide greater flexibility with the lighting layout. After getting a quote of $4,000 for professionally made doors, I decided I could make my own.

Carriage doors anyone can build— I wanted the doors to be lightweight, well insulated, and really rigid to resist sagging over time. True frame-and-panel construction didn't seem to be a good way to accomplish any of those tasks. Instead, I chose a torsion-box design consisting of a solid-wood frame with plywood on each face, similar to the way a hollow-core door is made. This would create a very rigid structure with plenty of room for insulation.

I started with a 1½-in.-thick poplar frame joined with stub tenons. Long tenons aren't necessary; in fact, biscuits would work fine, because all the strength comes from the plywood skins. I used a dado blade to cut a ½-in.-wide by 1-in.-deep groove in the frame parts. I also used the dado blade to cut stub tenons on the ends of the parts to fit the groove. The frame was glued and screwed through the tenons.

I filled the cavity with rigid insulation and glued and nailed plywood to each face. This created a very rigid torsion box that should resist sagging for many years. The outer face is ½-in. plywood while the inside face is ¼-in. plywood to help keep the weight down. I added windows and framed the outside face with ¾-in.-thick lumber for a frame-and-panel look similar to the other bay. The final result is a 48-in.-wide door that weighs less than a typical solid-oak entry door, and is far cheaper than a custom-built door. The guys at *Fine Homebuilding* were impressed.

I mounted the doors with long strap hinges that are plenty strong and look great. They were also very easy to install. First, I attached the hinges to the doors with lag screws. Then I set the doors in place using shims to locate them properly. With consistent gaps all around, I bolted the hinges to the door frame.

A wood floor is warm and easy on the feet

For the floor, I took a cue from a chapter on shop flooring by Scott Gibson (p. 68). I glued and nailed pressure-treated 2x4s to the concrete floor, placing rigid insulation in between. The insulation I used was the same thickness as the 2x4s, so I spaced the sleepers 24 in. on center. Normally a spacing of 16 in. would be necessary to prevent the floor from sagging under the weight of heavy machines, but since the rigid insulation has good compressive strength, 24 in. is fine. Before screwing the ¾-in. T&G (tongue-and-groove) plywood in place, I stapled 6-mil plastic over the insulation to act as a vapor barrier, just as Gibson recommended.

I moved as much as possible out of the shop by filling an 8-ft. by 12-ft. portable storage container (www.pods.com) that was dropped off in my driveway before construction started. Unfortunately, some machinery didn't fit, so I had to install the floor in two parts, moving the equipment from one side to the other. Installation would have been easier in an empty shop, but I was able to get the entire floor done in a day. The new floor is warmer, easier to sweep, and much kinder to my feet and joints.

Enclose the ceiling for a brighter, warmer shop

The ceiling posed a challenge. I like the looks and reflected light provided by an enclosed ceiling, but the bottom of my ceiling joists

Plywood floor adds warmth and comfort

A plywood floor installed over rigid insulation is easier on the knees and helps dampen noise and vibration from shop machines. Three coats of polyurethane protect the plywood from spills and wet shoes and make sweeping easier.

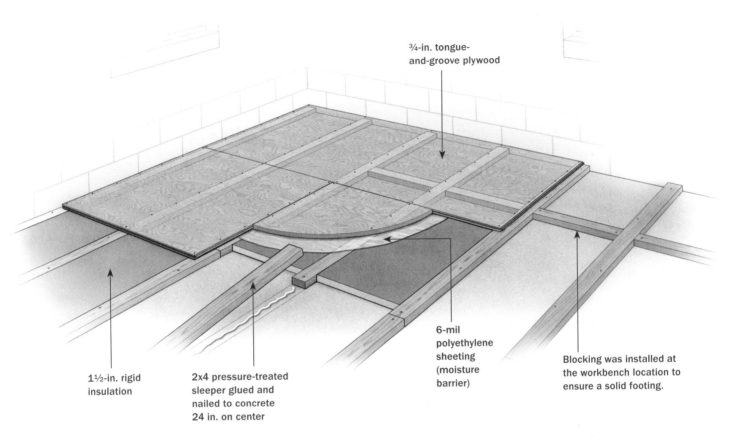

¾-in. tongue-and-groove plywood

6-mil polyethylene sheeting (moisture barrier)

1½-in. rigid insulation

2x4 pressure-treated sleeper glued and nailed to concrete 24 in. on center

Blocking was installed at the workbench location to ensure a solid footing.

Simple process. Working from one wall toward the opposite wall is an easy way to ensure the 2-ft. by 8-ft. foam panels and 2x4 pressure-treated sleepers fit tightly together. After applying a generous bead of construction adhesive (left), Pekovich uses fasteners from a powder-actuated tool to keep the sleeper in position while the glue sets (center). Then the whole floor is covered with a layer of 6-mil polyethylene and ¾-in. tongue-and-groove underlayment-grade plywood (right).

How to insulate concrete walls

To get the maximum insulation value, the first layer of insulation spans the wall without interruption and a second layer is fit between studs. Finally, a layer of ½-in. drywall painted white was placed on top, creating a bright and inviting workspace.

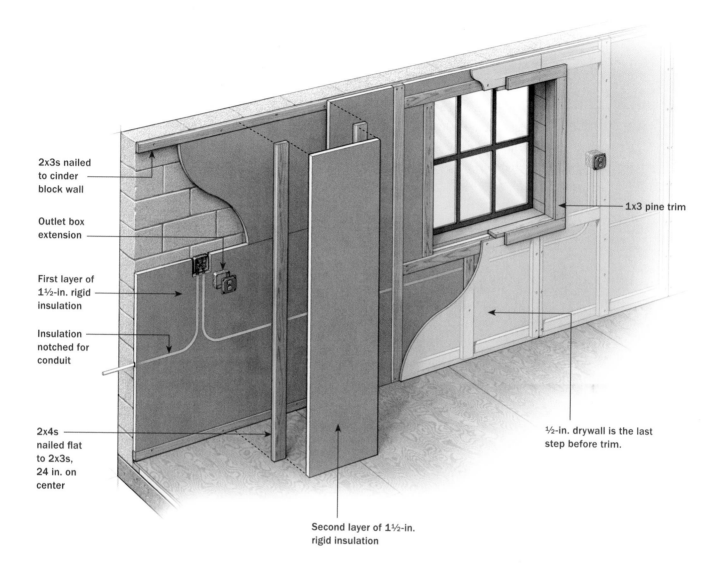

2x3s nailed to cinder block wall

Outlet box extension

First layer of 1½-in. rigid insulation

Insulation notched for conduit

2x4s nailed flat to 2x3s, 24 in. on center

Second layer of 1½-in. rigid insulation

1x3 pine trim

½-in. drywall is the last step before trim.

were now only 7½ ft. off my new plywood floor. The space felt more cramped and claustrophobic. My first thought was to spray insulation on the underside of the roof and leave the ceiling joists open. The insulation contractor said I'd still need to cover the insulation with plywood or drywall if the joists were left open, so I decided to look into raising the joists and enclosing the ceiling.

I spoke to the local building department about my situation and an engineer in the department concluded I could raise the ceiling joists 2 ft. without creating structural problems. I had always thought of building inspectors as something best avoided on small home-improvement jobs, but on this project, they were a big help.

Again, I'm a woodworker, not a carpenter, so the idea of raising ceiling joists was a little scary. Fortunately, the actual process wasn't that bad. I was able to reuse the existing joists by cutting them one at a time and nailing them in their new location (some local codes don't allow the reuse of materials, so check first). One smart thing I did was to rent a cordless Paslode® framing nailer from my local home center.

The final ceiling is a lofty 9 ft. While the floor plan didn't grow, the shop now has a more spacious feel, and by adding some ½-in. OSB (oriented strand board) on top of the ceiling joists, I have some much-needed storage above the ceiling. To access that space, I installed a fold-down attic ladder and wired a light in the attic. For insulation, I decided to spray the underside of the roof with open-cell foam insulation. Since my rafters are only 6 in. deep, I only was able to achieve an R20. But since foam practically eliminates air movement, which experts say

Wall insulation in two layers. With 2x4 nailers already installed top and bottom, the first layer of insulation is put up horizontally and then studs are turned sideways and placed on top. A second layer of insulation is fit between the studs. Use spray foam to seal any gaps between the framing and insulation.

is the real nemesis in heat loss, it should perform very well.

When it came time to reinstall the lights, I decided on an upgrade. I replaced my three old 8-ft. two-bulb fixtures with nine 4-ft. four-bulb fixtures, effectively tripling the amount of light in the shop. With the addition of the white ceiling and walls, my shop now glows like a beacon.

Basement approach to wall insulation

The walls of a typical frame-construction garage are easy to insulate. But the walls of my shop are concrete block, so I used an insulation method more suited to a basement shop, but with a modern twist. Rather than frame out the concrete wall in the typical fashion with studs on edge and the insulation in between, I took a different approach.

On the advice of Rob Wotzak, an expert on green construction at *Fine Homebuilding*, I started by covering the masonry wall with a continuous layer of rigid insulation, wedging it between a top and bottom plate that I nailed to the block wall. Over that, I attached the studs flat against the insulation, nailing them to the plates. From there, I

installed a second layer of insulation between the studs and finished with drywall. Installing the studs on edge would have created a thermal bridge from the block wall to the drywall, reducing the insulating properties of the wall. The continuous layer of insulation between the block wall and studs acts as a thermal break and should result in lower heating bills. The finished wall is only 3½ in. thick but boasts an R-value over 20.

A true transformation

What started as a long-overdue insulation job ended up as a completely transformed workspace. In replacing the doors, I wasn't looking to beautify my home, but the result is a quaint backyard shop that's bright and inviting.

It's not just the shop that has had a makeover. I've also picked up a few new skills. I've done some serious framing and remodeling. I've acquired new drywall skills and an appreciation for those people who do it well. Basic wiring is no longer a mystery to me. But, as much as I've enjoyed the new challenges, I'm happy to put my tool belt aside and get back to woodworking.

Smart Workshop, From the Ground Up

MATTHEW TEAGUE

When I left the staff of *Fine Woodworking* and headed south a few years ago, my wife and I bought a '50s ranch just east of downtown Nashville. I set up shop in the flat-roofed, one-car garage out back while we figured out if I could make a living building furniture and writing about the craft. Two years later, both careers were going well. The workshop, however, was growing smaller every day.

One year, from dream to reality

Between April 2006 and March 2007, Teague chronicled the process of building his shop. Here are a few milestones from the construction process:

June 23, 2006. They used only exterior forms for the foundation walls. As they worked their way around, they'd push the rock up against the concrete.

June 28, 2006. At the end of the day, I'm left with a handsome shop floor. Around dusk I like to stand out there and pretend I'm looking out my windows.

July 28, 2006. No matter how many times you've seen it, everyone wants to lend a hand raising the first wall.

August 9, 2006. A little sweat and a good push slide the trusses onto the top of the framing.

August 21, 2006. After the roof went on I was able to get both the electrician and the plumber to do their rough-in work while the building sat idle.

September 1, 2006. After all the trim was set in place, it took two days to wrap the building in HardiePlank siding with a 5-in. reveal.

October 26, 2006. Having recently drywalled a room's worth of ceiling in my own house, I had no hesitation hiring a crew to handle the shop.

November 19, 2006. For months now, I've waited for the day to move out of my old shop and into the new one . . . a short distance I must have walked a thousand times.

I didn't need an industrial shop for a big crew, but I did want a well-equipped workshop for a single pro, with plenty of bench space, versatile storage, adequate lighting, dust collection, and enough uncramped space to allow for tools and efficient workflow—the same requirements a serious hobbyist might have. I moved into my new shop recently, and the lessons I learned should be valuable to anyone thinking about building a small, detached shop for woodworking. Many of these tips also will work for updating an existing garage.

An architect is a good value

If you're building a shop and you're concerned about either its look or resale value, hiring an architect is worth the relatively small outlay of money (ours charged $560). In my case, he devised construction alternatives to raise the ceiling without raising the roof; he helped convince me—against the contractor's suggestion—to keep the bumped-out roof over the entry door; and he was available for last-minute phone calls to help solve the inevitable snafus that pop up during construction. Also, at least in my county, having full renderings of the building plan helped us skate past an otherwise overbearing inspection department. In short, if I had to do it again, I'd probably ask more of the architect instead of less.

For resale reasons, we designed the building to serve as a two-car garage, though we'll never park a car in it ourselves. And even if codes had allowed for a larger shop, I'd have stayed near the 700-sq.-ft. limit (we ended up at 698). Even on paper, anything larger looked like a monstrosity alongside our humble home.

The architect helped to ensure that the design complements our brick ranch house: He drew in a low-slung (4/12 pitch) hip roof like

Shop wainscoting. To add character and impact resistance, and to leave less area for drywalling, Teague nailed simple MDF wainscoting onto the stud walls. The stiles mark the studs, making it easier to hang things like this ledger board for the long work surface in the right rear corner.

A well-designed workshop

Teague tapped all of his experience from past shops he owned and the articles and books he worked on as a writer and editor to build and equip a safe, comfortable, well-organized garage shop.

PLENTY OF ROOM TO WORK

Two workbenches team up with a long utility bench in the other corner to provide plenty of room for projects, and the center of the shop floor is wide open for assembly and finishing.

the one on the house and then, to prevent the building from looking like a box with a cap, he set the front door in a small bump-out under a cantilevered roof. Though the house is brick, we opted for HardiePlank® siding on the shop and saved about $5,000.

While the architect worried mostly about the exterior of the shop, I spent countless hours sketching the interior. I wanted plenty of natural light inside, a comfortable office space, and, for waterstones and general cleanup, the luxury of running water. I settled on a half-bath (a toilet and a mop sink), with room for later expansion, combined with a small office for books and a computer—together the two rooms take up only 96 sq. ft. of space, but they save countless trips to the house.

With the office and bath in the back corner of the shop, I was left with a generous 600 sq. ft. of L-shaped shop space. Once we had a working drawing, I made scaled cutouts of all my tools and set them in place. Before we broke ground, I needed to know that everything would fit.

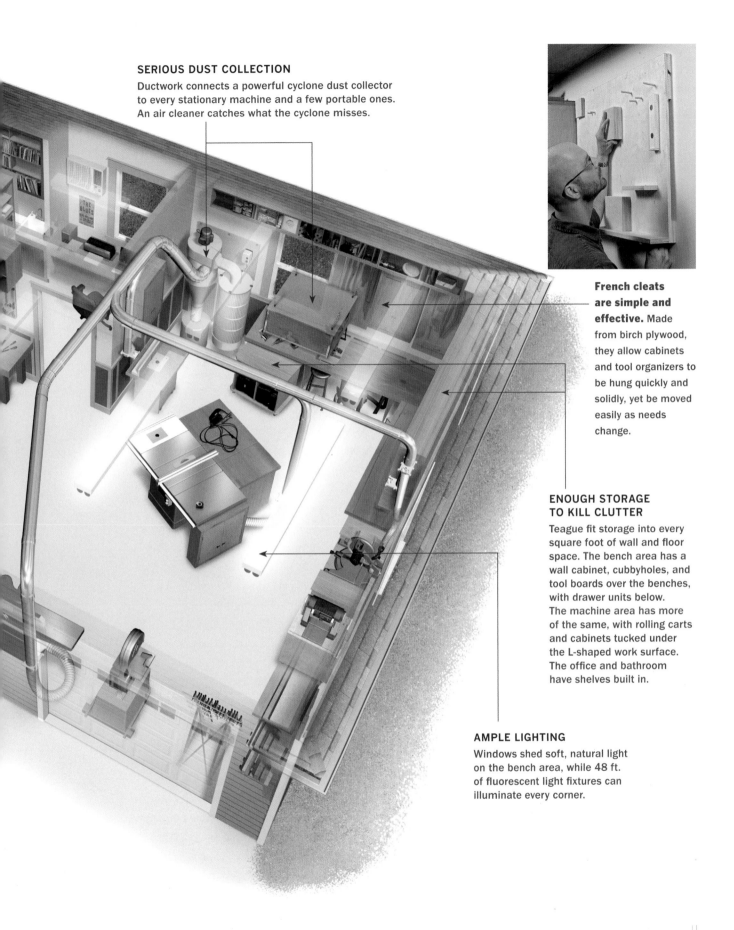

SERIOUS DUST COLLECTION

Ductwork connects a powerful cyclone dust collector to every stationary machine and a few portable ones. An air cleaner catches what the cyclone misses.

French cleats are simple and effective. Made from birch plywood, they allow cabinets and tool organizers to be hung quickly and solidly, yet be moved easily as needs change.

ENOUGH STORAGE TO KILL CLUTTER

Teague fit storage into every square foot of wall and floor space. The bench area has a wall cabinet, cubbyholes, and tool boards over the benches, with drawer units below. The machine area has more of the same, with rolling carts and cabinets tucked under the L-shaped work surface. The office and bathroom have shelves built in.

AMPLE LIGHTING

Windows shed soft, natural light on the bench area, while 48 ft. of fluorescent light fixtures can illuminate every corner.

Shop around for a builder

Construction bids from general contractors were at least $50,000. We then called a contractor who builds garages exclusively. His bid came in at just over half that of the cheapest general contractor. I checked out some of his work, called his references, and signed on.

The builder would be responsible for pouring the foundation, framing, roofing, and installing the windows and doors. I opted to subcontract the plumbing, electrical, insulation, drywall, and exterior painting myself. Being a nice guy, the builder even helped me negotiate lower prices with a few of the subs. In retrospect, I don't think I saved much money by subbing out work myself. When a contractor calls a sub he deals with every day, he gets a better price than you do when you ask them to squeeze a single job into a busy schedule.

What to DIY

As for what to do on my own, like many of you, I had to weigh what I was willing to do against how much money I could make working the same number of hours. In most cases, it was cheaper to hire out. Case in point: I was willing to buy rolls of insulation and install it myself. But at the behest of my builder I checked with a local insulation crew. They installed better insulation than I had planned to buy—and for about $350 less than I would have paid for materials alone. They showed up a day after I called them and were gone in an hour and a half. Better yet, I didn't itch at all.

As for enlisting the help of friends, on large construction jobs, you realize pretty soon that you'll need a crew of buddies for almost every task at hand. And since you can call on them only so often, you have to pick your battles. Consider this, too: If you can't get to a task immediately, it puts off all the

subcontractors in line behind you (you can't drywall until you install insulation, etc.). Even with all I subbed out, there were plenty of construction concerns to keep me busy.

In cases where the work was relaxing or really mattered to me, I did it myself. I built the cabinetry and storage units and did all of the trim work. I also installed the dust collector and ducting.

A great option for heating and cooling

I've worked in shops that aren't climate-controlled, and neither 20°F nor 100°F is very inspiring. Installing central heating and air seemed like a no-brainer. However, for a fraction of the price, a number of HVAC guys told me, an electric 15,000-Btu packaged terminal air conditioner (PTAC) would work as well. PTACs essentially are small heat pumps and are common in hotel rooms.

The framers left an opening for the unit, and the electrician ran an extra 220v outlet on a dedicated circuit. All I had to do was set the unit in the wall and plug it in. I spent a little extra to add a thermostat—a good decision. After paying the bills through a harsh winter and a Nashville summer, the PTAC seems just as efficient as the central heat-pump system we put in the house.

Electrical: More is more

My builder led me to an electrician who called back promptly, showed up when he said he would, and actually seemed to like what he does for a living. To boot, his prices were reasonable. He re-routed a 100-amp panel from the old shop and installed both 220v and 110v outlets everywhere I might want to place a tool; adding an outlet during construction costs only a few extra bucks but doing so later is both pricey and a hassle. For convenience, we located all of the outlets

42 in. off the floor—above bench height. He also supplied and installed six 8-ft. strips of fluorescent lighting.

Walls made for woodworking

Once the shell of the building was up, I did the bulk of the interior work, beginning with the extra-high walls. If I went with drywall from floor to ceiling, I worried that I'd punch countless holes in the walls as I moved boards around the shop. So I designed and installed medium-density fiberboard (MDF) wainscoting around the lower 40 in. of the walls—to just above bench height. I milled all of the trim pieces for windows, doors, and wainscoting from a few sheets of MDF, at a fraction of what off-the-shelf molding would have cost. I centered each wainscoting stile on a stud—when I hang cabinets on the wall, I don't need a stud finder.

Once the drywall contractors were done (I'm no fan of that job), I painted the top of the walls a light tan color; it masks dust and it's less bland than stark white. I painted the wainscoting panels red, but left the MDF trim natural with just a shellac finish.

As much as I'd prefer wood floors—they're much easier on your back and dropped tools—I had to draw the line somewhere. I sealed the concrete floor with a durable epoxy paint. In front of my workbenches and tablesaw I rolled out anti-fatigue floor mats.

Work flow: From machines to benches

In any efficient shop, work flow determines the tool layout. In my shop, raw lumber comes in the garage door and goes straight onto the lumber racks. With only slight tweaks, I used the lumber-rack design outlined by Andy Beasley (p. 168). Boards slide easily off the racks and onto the chopsaw, where I cut them to rough length. I then stack them on a mobile cart near the jointer, the planer, and the tablesaw. By the time I'm toting workpieces to the workbench, router table, or one of the work areas along the back and side walls, they're already milled to a manageable size.

Big tools first—To accommodate long boards, I set the tablesaw at an angle in the center of the shop, and behind it I put my old outfeed table that doubles as a storage unit. The tablesaw is also outfitted with a router table on the left extension wing. Having two router tables comes in handy when I'm using paired router bits. My main router table is located along the short wall opposite the office. It's built to the height of the tablesaw and rolls out to provide extra outfeed support.

I left both garage doors operable but realized that I'd only need access to one. A new 12-in. jointer (a shop-warming gift to myself) sits against the garage door I seldom use.

The bench area is an oasis—I didn't get into woodworking because I like heavy, loud machines. What I enjoy most is time at the workbench with hand tools. For that, I placed my two real workbenches in the smaller section of the shop. When I walk in the door, seeing the two walls of benches and hand tools makes me feel like I'm walking into a woodshop instead of a factory.

Storage and more storage

Whenever possible, I try to design storage into my workstations. My chopsaw stand is outfitted with shallow metal drawers available from Lee Valley (www.leevalley.com) that slide on grooves cut directly into cabinet sides. The outfeed table for the tablesaw holds my handheld power tools, and the auxiliary table sits on a cabinet for tablesaw accessories. All of the wall-storage units—including cabinets and tool boards—are hung on French cleats, making it easy to move or rearrange them later.

Let the work flow

The office/bathroom shortens one end of the shop, creating distinct areas for machine and bench work. Materials flow in the garage door, onto the lumber rack; through the nearby milling machines; onto the bandsaw, drill press, and router table; and then into the bench area for joinery, assembly, and finishing before heading out the way they came in.

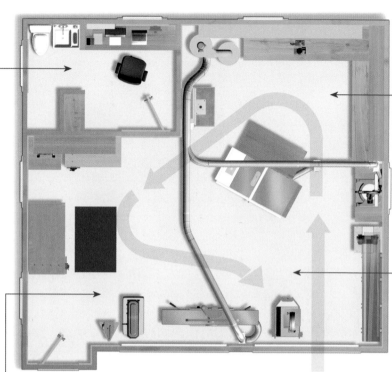

Comfort and self-sufficiency. An office for computer, stereo, and books, along with a small bathroom, keeps Teague on task all day long.

Hand-tool oasis. The smaller corner of the shop houses two real workbenches with storage for hand tools and hardware, and plenty of natural light.

Power central.
The larger portion of the shop consolidates the machines and dust-collection ducting, with plenty of lumber storage and all-purpose benchtop space around the outside.

Materials and milling. With the lumber rack built next to the garage door (above), Teague can move materials easily into the shop. The jointer and tablesaw are nearby (right) for milling, and a planer cart and lumber cart roll between them to complete an efficient array.

Long workbench accommodates roll-out carts—One of the best moves I made was to build a long work surface that starts at the chopsaw station, turns the corner at the back wall, and extends to the dust collector. The surface is simply two thicknesses of plywood glued and screwed together, and it's supported by ¾-in.-thick plywood panels instead of cabinet bases. Underneath I keep a low, rolling assembly table, as well as storage cabinets of various designs. I also keep my pancake-style compressor there, on its own rolling base.

At last, real dust collection

Because the shop shares space with my office, I wanted to keep dust to an absolute minimum. I could have gotten away with a few smaller mobile units for dust collection, but not only do they take up more space, they also have to be wrangled around the shop constantly. After consulting numerous experts and manufacturers, I went with a 3-hp, 2-stage cyclone collector from Oneida® Air Systems (www.oneida-air.com). I provided them with a drawing of the shop's floor plan, and they gave me a parts list and a drawing of the ductwork layout.

For the ductwork itself, I spent about twice the price of traditional materials in favor of quick-release ducting from Nordfab (www.nordfab.com). This ducting snaps together without tools and goes up in a frac-

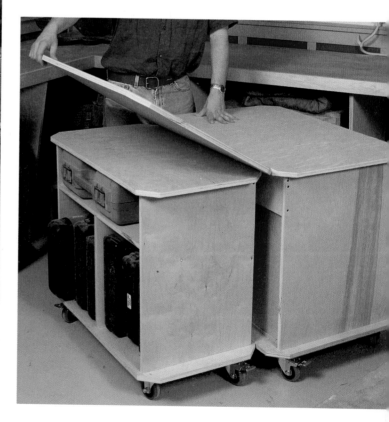

Rolling cart: storage and work space. Teague prefers an open-based bench with room for rolling carts below (above). One unit has simple drawers (top) that bring the tools to the job, with a hinged top that can flip onto another storage cart (right) to create a larger surface for assembly or finishing.

Bottom line: under $40K*

Not counting what I spent on tools and dust collection, which will move with me to my next shop, I came in under the $40,000 budget. It's worth noting that the shop is built on a pretty steep slope, which added a few thousand to the cost of the foundation.

*prices current in 2007

BUILDER Foundation, framing, siding, roofing, windows, and doors	$27,700
ARCHITECT	$560
PLUMBING Drain lines, water lines, and fixtures	$4,040
ELECTRICAL 100-amp panel, wiring, outlets, lighting	$3,440
INSULATION R-30 in the ceiling, R-19 in the walls	$650
DRYWALL	$850
EXTERIOR PAINTING	$1,200
CLIMATE CONTROL PTAC unit	$700
TRIM AND WAINSCOTING MATERIALS	$300
TOTAL	$39,440

tion of the time it takes to rivet and route traditional ductwork. Better still, it can be disassembled and rearranged easily should my tooling or layout change.

Even with a great dust-collection system, a little bit of dust is inevitable. To help manage airborne dust, I hung an air cleaner over the tablesaw. The cost was minimal, but it makes a noticeable difference.

Now that the shop is done and I've spent a few months building furniture there, I don't miss the few corners I cut, but I do appreciate all the extras I insisted on. The floor paint, wainscoting, half-bath, top-flight dust collection, and smart storage solutions all work together to create a comfortable and inspiring workspace. When I walk through the door each morning, I know I'm set up to build almost anything that pops into my mind. It's become my home a few feet away from home.

DIY ducting in a day. Teague spent a lot more to get Nordfab ducting, which goes together in a toolless snap and can be dismantled and rearranged just as easily. Oneida, the cyclone manufacturer, eased the process further by producing a ductwork diagram and parts list, based on a drawing of the floor plan.

Rolling, rotating planer cart

Planers require a lot of infeed and outfeed space, so I've always stored my benchtop planer on a cart under the right wing of my tablesaw, pulling it out when I needed it. But that meant either lifting the heavy planer onto a benchtop or working crouched over. In this shop, I've found a better way.

A pivoting-top tool station is not a new idea, but this one works especially well and is easy to build. The planer is bolted to a top that spins on a ½-in. steel rod.

For support at the chopsaw, I simply screwed a length of hard maple to the other side of the top. A more versatile option would be to install an adjustable roller on the side of the cabinet. Then I could use the other side of the top for another tool, such as a disk/belt sander combination.

The secret is to start by building the top and then size the cabinet parts to fit it. The top is two ¾-in.-thick pieces of birch plywood glued onto an inner hardwood frame, creating a torsion box of sorts. The frame is the exact thickness of the steel rod, and its two halves are positioned snugly against the rod so it is supported on four sides. The pivot mechanism is deceptively simple: The top is edged with maple, and the rod passes through that edging, ending in two support strips that sit atop the cabinet sides. Before attaching the side edging to the top, drill a ½-in. hole through its center points. Then glue on the edging with the rod in place. Now slide two washers onto each end of the steel rod, and epoxy the rod into the outer support strips.

Another innovative cart. The pivoting-top planer cart spends most of its life as an outfeed support for the chopsaw (top right), with the planer lying in wait. When needed, the planer pivots upward (center right), where it uses the top of the tablesaw for outfeed support (bottom right).

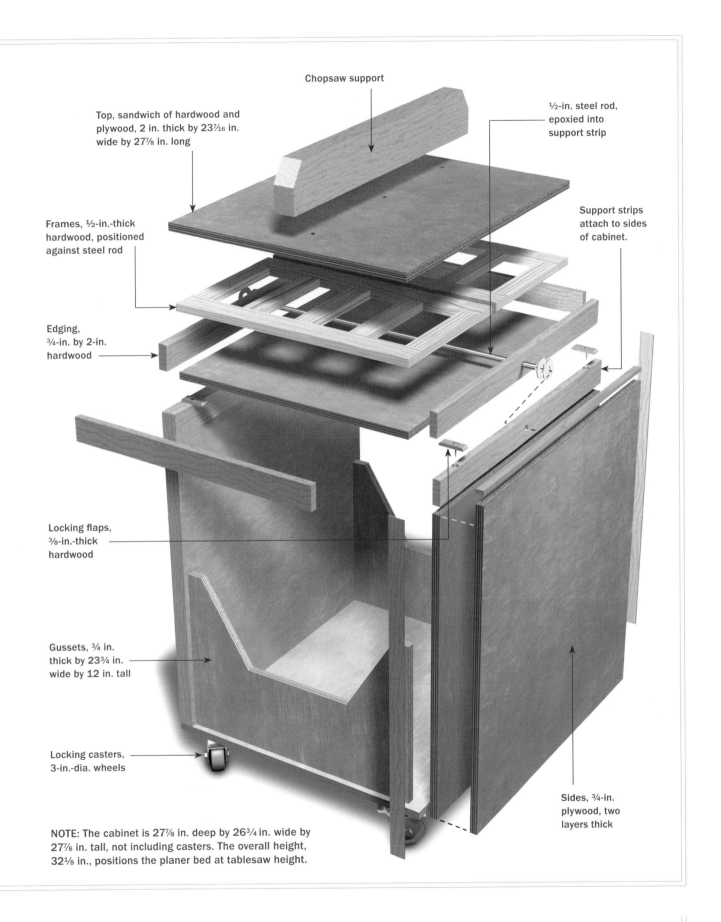

Chopsaw support

Top, sandwich of hardwood and plywood, 2 in. thick by 23⁷⁄₁₆ in. wide by 27⅞ in. long

½-in. steel rod, epoxied into support strip

Frames, ½-in.-thick hardwood, positioned against steel rod

Support strips attach to sides of cabinet.

Edging, ¾-in. by 2-in. hardwood

Locking flaps, ⅜-in.-thick hardwood

Gussets, ¾ in. thick by 23¾ in. wide by 12 in. tall

Locking casters, 3-in.-dia. wheels

Sides, ¾-in. plywood, two layers thick

NOTE: The cabinet is 27⅞ in. deep by 26¾ in. wide by 27⅞ in. tall, not including casters. The overall height, 32⅛ in., positions the planer bed at tablesaw height.

A Shop for a Small Space

STELIOS L.A. STAVRINIDES

At the very least, starting a woodworking shop requires two things: good woodworking tools and adequate space. Where I live, on the Mediterranean island of Cyprus, both are in short supply.

But I love woodworking, and I didn't want to let these problems stand in my way. So, using SketchUp®, I designed a fully function-ing shop that would fit into a 5-ft. by 5-ft. storage room when not in use.

To make it work, I converted the portable power tools I already had into stationary machines, mounting them on a compact, rolling bench. This bench houses five major tools: tablesaw, router table, jigsaw, drill press, and disk sander. And it leaves plenty of space in my storeroom for lumber and other tools.

Of course, the shop has limits. I don't have a jointer or a planer, so I have to start with stock that is already jointed flat and milled to thickness. Also, the tools must be rolled out into the covered parking area of my apartment complex for use. It's not good for cold weather, but fortunately, we have very little of that here.

Apart from those drawbacks, my little shop can do a lot of woodworking. Here's a look at how it works.

How to fit a whole hobby into a 5x5 closet

I pack all of my woodworking tools and supplies into a storage room in the parking area of my apartment building. The room measures approximately 5 ft. square and 8 ft. high—a little more than twice the volume

Rolling workstation is the key. The power-tool station rides on casters, so it rolls easily out of its storage area. After connecting to a nearby power outlet, Stavrinides is ready to begin work on any of five power tools.

A shop in a closet

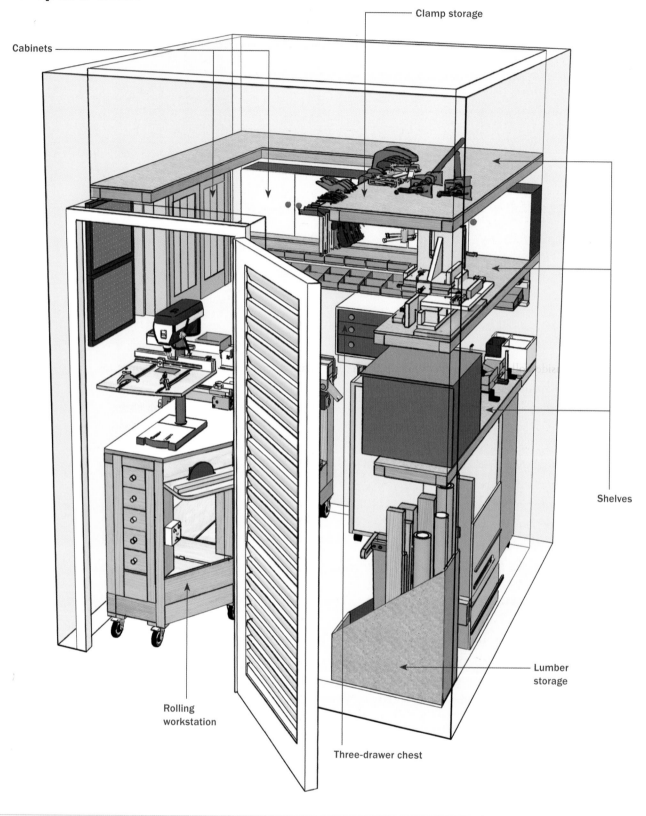

Clamp storage

Cabinets

Shelves

Lumber storage

Rolling workstation

Three-drawer chest

A cabinet in a cabinet. Interior doors provide space to hang more tools inside this rolling storage piece, which measures 32 in. square by 13 in. deep. To get the most out of the space, Stavrinides planned the tool layout on paper first.

inside Volkswagen's modern Beetle. With such a tight fit, one end of the cart that serves as my rolling workstation is angled to allow access into the space.

An old, narrow bookcase mounted horizontally and fitted with doors holds fasteners, glue, finishing supplies, and safety gear. The larger, wall-mounted cabinet is stocked with router bits, featherboards, hold-down clamps, and miscellaneous gear.

The top drawer in my three-door chest is for sketches, computer printouts, and woodworking plans. The middle drawer holds tool manuals and small accessories that come with the tools. The bottom drawer provides storage for sandpaper of all types—sheets, circular pads, and rolls.

Three levels of shelves wrap around three walls to provide storage space for lumber, hardware, supplies, a first-aid kit, and other tools including power drills, a biscuit joiner, and a mortising attachment for the drill press.

A section of upper shelf serves as a rack for C-clamps and small pistol-grip clamps.

Larger pipe clamps and parallel clamps are stored flat on the shelf itself. In all, the space holds about 65 clamps of varying types.

For lumber storage, a narrow box with an angled, open top holds cutoffs of varying lengths and tucks under the lower shelf.

Rolling workstation: The big idea inside the small shop

I designed a power-tool bench on wheels to serve multiple functions and fit inside my storage space. The bench, 20 in. wide by 59 in. long, is built on a frame of 2x4 and 2x2 lumber, with a plywood skin and a ¾-in. MDF top surfaced with plastic laminate for durability. A 7¼-in. circular saw is bolted under the bench, but it can be removed to handle large sheet goods. In addition to the power tools, the bench also features a vise, five small drawers for accessories, and eight electrical sockets.

The rip fence is shopmade of MDF and serves both the tablesaw and the router table.

Rolling workstation

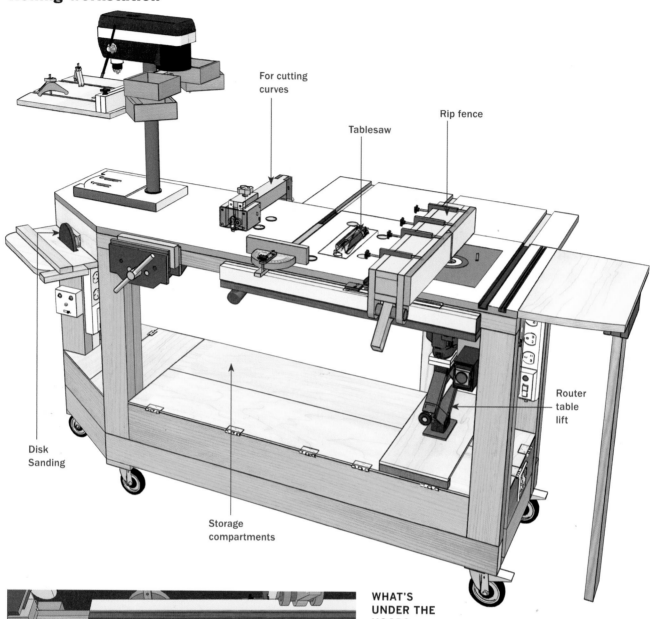

For cutting curves

Tablesaw

Rip fence

Disk Sanding

Storage compartments

Router table lift

WHAT'S UNDER THE HOOD?

A table-mounted array of portable power tools serve as standard shop machines. Shown here are the jigsaw, circular saw, and router.

The power-tool bench at work

Stavrinides used the tablesaw, jigsaw, and sanding station in his rolling bench to create a router template for a decorative drawer front. He then used the template to shape the workpiece on the router table.

The circular saw yields straight, clean cuts. Note that the rip fence doubles as a router-table fence and includes dust collection.

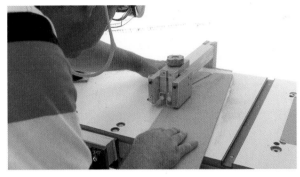

For curves, the inverted jigsaw. Stavrinides recommends investing in high-quality blades. His shopmade guide assembly keeps the blade straight and vertical during the cut.

Fair the curve at the sanding station. A flip-up table supports the work. The sanding attachment uses hook-and-loop pads and is powered by a variable-speed electric drill.

Shape the workpiece at the router table. The author's version doesn't have through-the-table height adjustment, relying on automotive technology instead (see drawing on the facing page).

Separate fence faces for the router are secured with fence clamps (www.rockler.com) and removed for tablesaw use.

The scissor jack from my Alfa Romeo serves as a router-lift mechanism that is precise to a millimeter. The wooden pad on which the router rests is relieved slightly to let air circulate over the motor vents.

The disk-sanding attachment is powered by an electric drill with its controls (on/off,

forward/reverse, variable speed) rewired to a bench-mounted control panel.

I use a bench-mounted jigsaw instead of a bandsaw or scrollsaw for cutting curves. An arm-mounted guide uses a pair of roller bearings to keep the blade from wandering in the cut.

Lastly, the built-in storage bins underneath provide space for tool accessories, extension cords, and small pieces of lumber.

Wiring a Workshop

CLIFFORD A. POPEJOY

The electrical wiring, outlets, and lighting in your shop should be as specialized as your tools. It's hard to turn out high-quality work—or to work safely—in a poorly illuminated shop. It is equally frustrating and potentially dangerous if your tools keep tripping breakers on underpowered circuits or if your floor is a tangle of extension cords. To upgrade your workspace to meet the special needs of woodworking, you should know how to identify your needs and then communicate them to an electrician with the skills to turn your plan into reality. If you put these ideas to use, your woodworking will be safer and more satisfying.

Shop features dictate the wiring layout

Installing the wiring for a woodshop is done most easily during construction or remodeling with the walls open, but it can be done anytime. If the walls are closed in, either have the wiring run in surface-mounted conduit or hire an "old work" electrician who can run wires in existing walls and make a minimum of holes to be patched later.

To feed the shop circuits, the best approach is to install an electrical subpanel (breaker box) specifically for the shop. In a well-designed system, a breaker will rarely trip, but if it does, it helps to have the panel nearby.

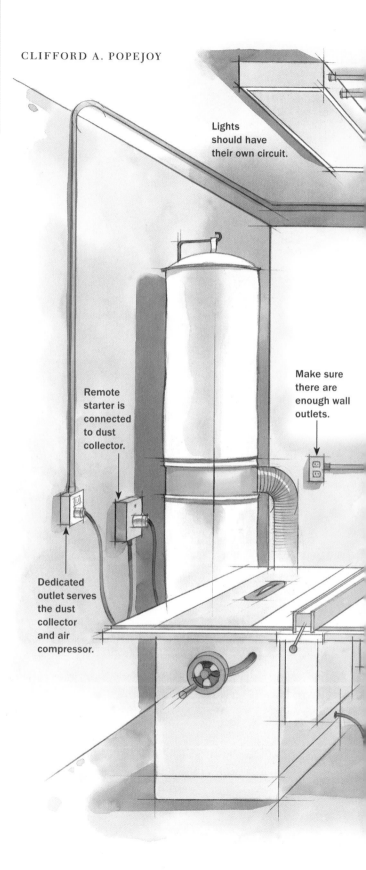

Lights should have their own circuit.

Make sure there are enough wall outlets.

Remote starter is connected to dust collector.

Dedicated outlet serves the dust collector and air compressor.

A boost in safety and convenience

Think about how you work, then plan to have ample power exactly where you need it.
The right array of circuits, switches, and outlets makes the shop more pleasant to work in,
and a few key accessories complete the picture.

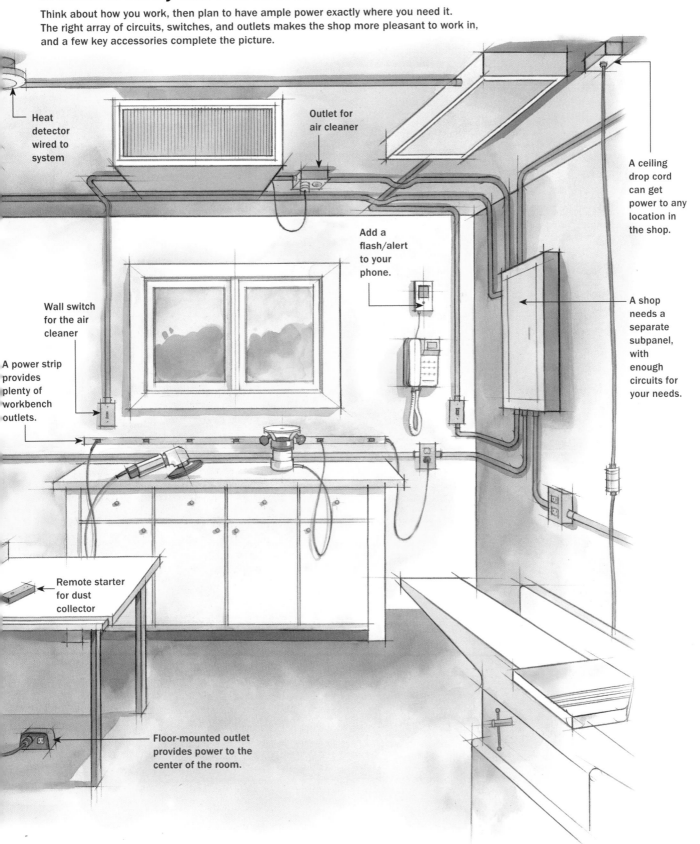

Heat detector wired to system

Outlet for air cleaner

A ceiling drop cord can get power to any location in the shop.

Add a flash/alert to your phone.

A shop needs a separate subpanel, with enough circuits for your needs.

Wall switch for the air cleaner

A power strip provides plenty of workbench outlets.

Remote starter for dust collector

Floor-mounted outlet provides power to the center of the room.

Plan circuit by circuit

Designing the wiring for your shop is pretty simple if you approach it piece by piece. Start by determining your lighting needs, then provide power for receptacles serving portable power tools. Finally, work out the requirements for stationary machines that might run simultaneously.

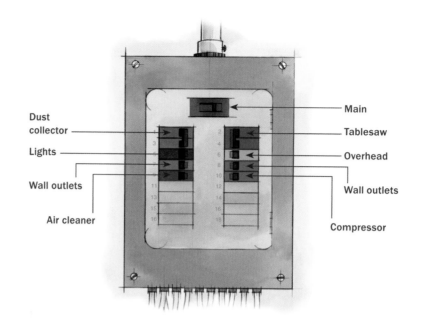

Dust collector
Lights
Wall outlets
Air cleaner

Main
Tablesaw
Overhead
Wall outlets
Compressor

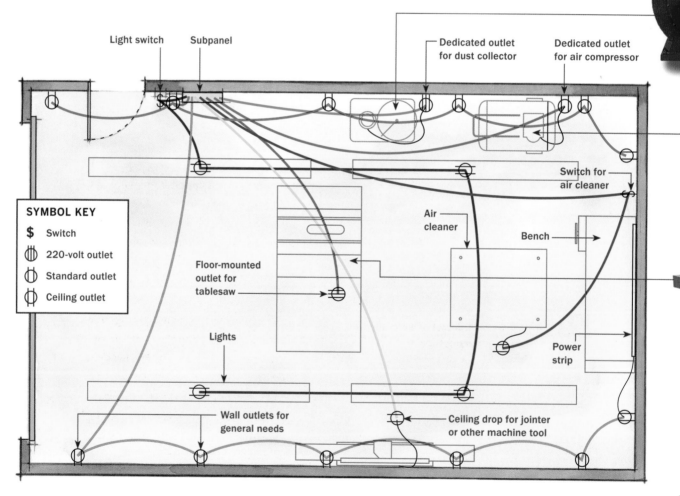

Light switch

Subpanel

Dedicated outlet for dust collector

Dedicated outlet for air compressor

Switch for air cleaner

Air cleaner

Bench

SYMBOL KEY

$ Switch

220-volt outlet

Standard outlet

Ceiling outlet

Floor-mounted outlet for tablesaw

Power strip

Lights

Wall outlets for general needs

Ceiling drop for jointer or other machine tool

Dust collector needs dedicated power. Check the voltage that the dust collector motor runs on, and wire a separate circuit for it.

Consider a separate circuit for the compressor. By running your air compressor on its own circuit, you avoid the possibility that it will trip a circuit breaker when another tool is used.

Cabinet saws have special needs. Create a separate 220v circuit, and run it to a floor outlet in the center of the shop.

There's a wide range of subpanels available, and your choice will depend on how much power and how many circuits you need.

At any given time, most one-person shops will be running one major stationary tool, a dust collector, an air filtration system, and lights. In this case, 60 amps at 240/120 volts likely will provide enough power. If there's heating or air conditioning running as well, a 100-amp subpanel probably will be adequate. I suggest a panel with room for 16 or 20 circuit breakers. These are starting points. Because each shop is different, you should calculate the number of circuits and power needs of your own.

There are two interdependent aspects to wiring a shop. One is circuit design—how the various things that use power (called "loads") are arranged and grouped, and how they are connected to their electricity source through wiring and circuit breakers. The other is the choice and location of light fixtures, receptacles, and switches.

Let there be light (on its own circuit)

Depending on the size of the shop, you should have one or more 120v, 15-amp circuits dedicated to lighting. That way if you are ripping a board and your tablesaw trips a breaker, you won't be plunged into darkness and into a dangerous situation.

To compute how many lighting circuits you will need, add up the total wattage of the lights and provide one 15-amp lighting circuit for every 1,500 watts. This is based on loading each circuit to about 80% of its capacity. This cushion, though not required in noncommercial applications, is still a good idea.

For example, to provide lighting for a single-car garage-size shop (240 sq. ft.) with 96-in., high-output (HO) fluorescent lights, you would need four separate 2-lamp fixtures. Each 8-ft. lamp requires 110 watts, so you would need a total of 880 watts to light this shop. Consider installing some task lighting (say a track fixture with three, 65-watt floodlamps or equivalent fluorescent floods) as well. I'd put this lighting on one 15-amp circuit.

Consider setting up the lighting so that the general lighting fixtures are wired to two or more separate switches, with the task lights switched separately from the general lighting. This way, if your machine and bench areas are separate, you can save energy by illuminating only the area in which you're working.

Outlets: the more the better

It's a fact that a shop can never have too many clamps, and it's equally true that it can't have too many receptacles. Receptacles should go on 20-amp circuits. There's no limit set by the National Electrical Code® (NEC) for the number of outlets that can go on a circuit in a residential application.

For a shop, it makes sense to identify the loads you expect to operate at the same time and group the receptacles onto circuits so that each circuit can comfortably support the expected demand. A 120v, 20-amp circuit can provide 2,400 watts, although it's a good idea to keep the load to 80% or less, or about 1,900 watts. To figure out how many circuits are needed, look at the power needed as shown on the tool nameplate (some nameplates will specify watts, and some amps). If the tool specs give amps only, convert from amps to watts for a 120v tool by multiplying amps times 120. For instance, if you have a small air compressor that draws 13 amps (1,560 watts), put in a receptacle supplied by its own 20-amp circuit, called a "dedicated" circuit. For outlets that won't be supplying a specific

tool, as in an area like an assembly bench where you will be using various small power tools, I suggest three or four outlets on a 20-amp circuit.

The NEC requires ground fault circuit interrupter (GFCI) protection for any 15-amp or 20-amp branch circuits supplying a garage or other work area at grade level. You can meet this requirement by using a GFCI circuit breaker or by having a GFCI receptacle first in line and wired to protect the downstream receptacles.

For general-use outlets, like the ones used for routers, hand sanders, and corded drills, it is a good idea to set up circuits based on the area served. For example, you might set up a separate circuit for each wall. Or you may want a couple of 20-amp circuits to serve your workbench, where you might have three or four outlets on each circuit. A neat trick is to run two circuits along the wall and feed alternating receptacles from the two different circuits. Don't use a shared neutral circuit for this; you have to GFCI-protect the outlets, and keeping the two circuits completely separate makes this easier.

A product called Plugmold® (www. wiremold.com) is useful for providing work-bench power. It is a steel channel with outlets spaced at intervals. Plugmold stands about 1¼ in. wide and proud of the surface and is available in various receptacle spacings (12 in. is best for shop use). Plugmold is much sturdier than a typical cord-connected "power strip" and is the right way to pack a lot of outlets along a wall.

It's a good idea to place wall outlets 50 in. above the floor (to the bottom of the box). That way, if you lean sheet goods against the wall, they won't cover the outlets, and the outlets will be well above any benchtop or other work surface. Another nice setup is to set aside a shelf area for cordless-tool chargers,

Get the power where you need it: ceiling . . .

One way to avoid having power cords strewn about your shop floor is to use a ceiling-mounted drop cord. This brings power to the middle of your shop in a convenient and safe way. Just roll out the tool of choice and plug away.

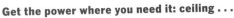

. . . or floor.

Another way to bring power to the middle of your shop is to use a monument-style receptacle. This type avoids the problems of a flush-mounted receptacle, which include dust clogging and possible shorts from metal objects.

Workbench power. A Plugmold power strip gives you a convenient place to plug in power tools that are used often at your workbench.

and put a 3-ft.-plus strip of Plugmold with 6-in. receptacle spacing on the wall behind the shelf. Put this on a separate 20-amp circuit, so you can leave it powered up while turning the other receptacle circuits off at the breakers for safety when you're not in the shop.

Get plenty of juice to stationary tools

The big guns—stationary tablesaw, jointer, planer, dust collector—draw so much power that they each require their own circuit. (Without it, running two simultaneously will trip a breaker.) If the motor can be set up to run on 240v, have an electrician do it. It will probably require taking the motor out of the machine. There's no power efficiency advantage to running a machine at 240v vs. 120v in a single-phase system, but the higher voltage means lower amperage, and as a result, you can use smaller-gauge power-supply wiring. That translates into less expense to run the wire and to hook it up.

To figure out what size circuits you will need, check the amp rating on each tool's data plate or in its product manual. Keep in mind that the circuit breaker at the subpanel is designed to protect the building's wiring from an overcurrent condition—it does not, however, ensure that the machine's motor won't overload. If the motor does not have an internal circuit breaker for overload protection (the tool manual will indicate this), a fused disconnect may be required. Ask the electrician to install it. The fuses in the disconnect box will protect the motor windings from overheating.

Some tools are an island—Getting power to a machine in the middle of the floor can be a challenge. You don't want a cord running along the floor that you might trip over. If there's a basement or crawlspace below, I would run cable or conduit below the floor and use a monument-style housing to hold the receptacle at the base of the machine (see center photo on p. 49). A flush-mounted floor outlet is a poor choice for a shop. It will fill with debris and could be shorted out by a stray nail or staple.

If you plan to move shop machines around and you want to keep the floor clear, use a hanging (pendant) outlet about 6 ft. to 7 ft. above the floor. To prevent accidental unplugging, a locking cord cap on the receptacle end of the pendant outlet is a good idea (see top photo on p. 49). This will require you to put a

Heat detector. Airborne wood dust can cause false alarms with a standard smoke detector. A heat detector can warn you of a shop fire and can be wired into your home fire-detection system if the shop is in a detached building.

Remote-control transmitter switch. A remote-control receiver is connected between the dust collector's power cord and the receptacle. A small transmitter lets you turn the collector on and off from anywhere in the shop. This will save you a few steps and let you devote more attention to your work.

compatible locking plug on the machine cord or to make an adapter.

Custom touches add safety, convenience

Even though they are full of flammable materials, most woodshops have no smoke alarms. That is because airborne sawdust can set off the photoionization or photoelectric sensors typically used in smoke alarms to detect smoke. The solution is to install a heat-detecting fire alarm that can activate the smoke alarms in the house.

It's nice to have a phone in the shop, but how do you hear it ring while planing boards and wearing hearing protectors? You can add a flashing visual alert.

Another convenience is to have your dust collector start automatically when you switch on a machine it serves. It's possible to build a current sensor/relay setup, but there are commercially available ones. Ecogate® (www.ecogate.com) sells a system that not only turns on the dust collector when it senses that a tool has started, but also opens and closes the adjacent blast gate. Alternatively, you could install a relay and receiver on the dust collector's cord that switches on and off with a remote-control transmitter that can sit in a convenient spot or hang on your key ring (like a car-door remote).

Work with your electrician

Unless you're a qualified electrician or are willing to take the time to become familiar with the techniques of the trade, the many requirements of the NEC, and any local codes pertinent to shop wiring, you should find a licensed electrician or electrical contractor to wire your shop. Look for one who does both residential and commercial work; a strictly residential electrician might not be familiar with some of the products and design elements suggested here.

When working with an electrician, it's more productive to explain the objective or goal than to try to dictate a precise method or approach. Sit down with the electrician before work begins, and lay out your requirements clearly. If your plan and goals are not clear at the outset, be prepared to pay for changes.

Finally, don't expect to find an electrician who will "just do the hookups" after you've pulled the wires, etc. Few licensed electricians will take the risk of putting the finishing touches on work they didn't do themselves.

Let There Be Light

NANCY McCOY AND PETER JUDGE

Have you ever had to squint to see a scribe line or line up a pencil mark? Maybe a recent finish looked great in the shop, but once you brought it into the house you found sanding scratches. Your problem might be inadequate shop lighting. Light fixtures are seldom at the top of tool and equipment wish lists, so most home shops are illuminated with a collection of mismatched, outdated fixtures, with little thought given to their overall placement and how they're switched.

As a result, improving your shop lighting will likely mean starting over with new wiring and fixtures. Many woodworkers will think they can handle this job, but it's probably better to hire an electrician who'll let you do some of the work yourself.

An electrician looking at the job can confirm that your electrical panel isn't overtaxed and that there are no other pressing electrical problems. Then you can save some money by mounting the fixtures and running the conduit yourself. Later, the electrician can check your work, run the wires, and make the connections inside the panel. Some electricians are fine with this type of arrangement. Others will want to do everything themselves, so make sure you work out the division of labor in advance.

We used *Fine Woodworking* associate editor Matt Kenney's shop to demonstrate the

Add a couple of task lights. Sanding and finishing may require smaller, directed lights.

BEFORE

AFTER

Lots of ambient light is the key. Home shops are commonly lit with 30 foot-candles or less (right), but 75 foot-candles is a better target (above). Installing a broad array of fluorescent fixtures will ensure that every corner of your shop has plenty of light.

Fluorescents are the foundation. Light every corner of a workshop—you never know where you might need a clear view. Overhead fluorescents arranged on a grid are the most cost-effective way to create a blanket of bright light.

Shop-ready fixtures. Modern fluorescents are the obvious choice for shop lighting. They have electronic ballasts that don't hum or flicker, and they're energy-efficient and affordable. The SB 432 from Lithonia (www.lithonia.com) has a wraparound lens that keeps out dust and spreads the light.

Lower-cost option. Strip (no lens) fluorescents are sold in 2-, 4-, and 8-ft. lengths. If you choose 8-footers, make sure to get them with pairs of 4-ft. bulbs instead of 8-ft. bulbs, which are harder to find and transport.

CHERRY UNDER
INCANDESCENT LIGHT

CHERRY UNDER
3000 K FLUORESCENT

techniques discussed in this article. Like most woodworkers, Matt thought his shop lighting was just fine. But when the upgrade was finished, he was amazed: "I don't have to get my eyes right up to the work to see what I'm doing anymore. More light just makes everything easier." The lighting upgrade also allowed Matt to start using the entire shop instead of the single well-lit area near his bench. Matt and local electrician Steve Foss worked together on the installation, with Matt installing the fixtures and Steve doing the wiring.

Two types of lighting

Any discussion of artificial light starts with the distinction between ambient and task lighting—you'll want both types for a well-lit shop. Ambient lighting describes general lighting for common cutting and shaping tasks. Task lighting describes a higher level of illumination focused right on the work. However, it's important to remember that once you have an even blanket of bright light, task lighting is reserved for filling in the dark areas.

Don't skimp—It might be tempting to save money on lighting by arranging the ambient overhead lights so that they're strategically placed over benches and machines. But we recommend against this approach because the lights will be in the wrong locations if you ever decide to change your shop setup.

And you never know quite where you'll need light: Will it be on the floor when cutting up a sheet of plywood or in the corner when picking through the scrap pile? With an even blanket of ambient light, you'll be able to work anywhere. You can save the task lighting for when you really need it, like finishing and joinery.

The Illuminating Engineering Society of North America (IES) recommends between 20 and 50 foot-candles for woodworking. One foot-candle is the amount of light produced by an ordinary candle measured from 1 ft. away. We suggest 75 foot-candles because you'll need more light as you age, and the cost difference is negligible. Even if your eyes are fine now, you'll need the additional light soon enough.

Light-colored surfaces boost light—Another consideration is how much of the light produced by your fixtures is reflected by the ceiling and walls. A clean, white surface may reflect as much as 85% of the light that

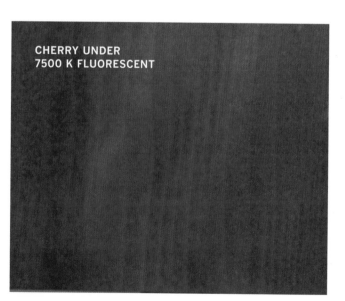

CHERRY UNDER
7500 K FLUORESCENT

True colors. A bulb's color temperature can make a big difference in the appearance of wood species and finishes. Ideally, you should select bulbs rated 3000 K, so the shop lighting matches your home lighting. Color temperature is found on packaging and sometimes right on the bulb.

Lay out lights for complete coverage. An electrician can help you determine the necessary fixtures and their placement. If you provide your own layout, be sure to ask if moving things a little or rotating the whole layout 90° will make the job easier and less expensive.

initially hits it, while a dark, rough surface can reflect as little as 10% or 15%. If your shop is cluttered and dusty or has exposed insulation, you'll need to boost lighting levels by another 30% to 50%, compared to shops with clean, white walls and ceilings.

A functional lighting layout is simple

Once you've made a decision on the level of lighting you want in your workshop, laying it out is as easy as 1-2-3.

1. Choose your fixture—The most common shop fixture is an open "strip" fluorescent (see top right photo on p. 54). These work pretty well, but without a cover, they experience more "dirt depreciation," which is the drop in light output caused by dust on the bulbs and housing. It's easy enough to clean off the fixtures once in a while with compressed air, but it's even easier to select fixtures with an acrylic lens. Not only does

the lens keep out much of the dust and spread the light, but it also provides a bit of safety when you're swinging around long boards.

Our favorite fixture for a home workshop is Model SB 432 from Lithonia Lighting® (see p. 54). These fixtures have a lens, and their electronic ballast means they won't hum loudly and they'll work in cold temperatures. They used to cost about 25% more than strip fluorescents, but we found them at www.Amazon.com for the same as or less than some strip lights.

2. Select the bulbs—One of the complaints we often hear about fluorescent bulbs is that the light is bluish and unnatural. This used to be true, but fluorescent bulbs are now available in a wide variety of "color temperatures." Measured in kelvins (K), color temperatures of fluorescent lights commonly range from 2000 K (warm red) to 7500 K (cool blue).

Why is a bulb's color temperature important? Ideally, the lighting in the shop should be the same as the lighting inside your home, so your projects look the same in both environments. Most likely you have warm incandescent lighting in your home, so you should select warm fluorescent bulbs with a 3000 K color temperature. This will help your finished projects look the way you intended, and the cost difference compared to standard bulbs is negligible.

3. Plan your layout—Most electricians and lighting showrooms can provide a lighting layout for a garage shop easily, but if you want to do the layout yourself, we suggest

Free layout software

Visual (www.lithonia.com) is a free lighting design program. Once you've entered the shop dimensions and selected a fixture from a pull-down menu, the software generates a layout based on the foot-candle requirement.

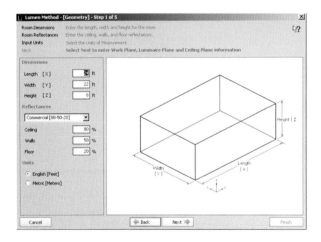

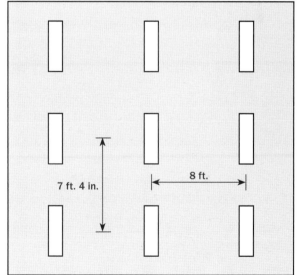

Sample solution. The lighting layout at right is for a two-car garage shop (22 ft. by 24 ft.) using 4-ft.-long, 4-bulb fixtures.

Hang your own fixtures.
Fluorescent fixtures are surprisingly light, so toggle bolts let you put them wherever you want on a drywall ceiling (above). You also can fasten the lights directly to framing members with screws. Another task you can do yourself is to install the straight conduit between fixtures (left). Before tightening the toggles or screws completely, use the wiggle room to squeeze in the pipe. Always be sure to ream the conduit ends, as any sharp edges will damage the wires' insulation.

using Visual™, a free program found on the Lithonia Web site (www.lithonia.com). Start the program by entering the shop dimensions and ceiling height, then specify a lighting level (75 foot-candles in our case). The program then gives you several options on the reflectivity of your walls. You can then select a light fixture from a pull-down menu, choose the type of ceiling and lens cover, and the software will tell you how many fixtures you need and how to arrange them.

Using the SB 432 fixture and assuming a 22-ft. by 24-ft. two-car-garage shop with 8-ft. ceilings as an example, the program

Leave the wiring to a pro. With the fixtures placed, you can bring back the electrician to install the rest of the conduit, run the wire, and make the necessary connections. This will likely take a day or less.

says we need nine fixtures, arranged in three columns of three fixtures each (see drawing on p. 57).

Zoning saves money and energy—Rather than having all your lights controlled by a single switch, it's a good idea to divide the space into work zones. For example, you could put the finishing table in one zone, the bench or assembly table in another, and the machine area in a third. For the cost of a little extra cable and a few switches, the energy savings are well worth it.

Another nice feature is an occupancy sensor that turns on a single light whenever you walk into the shop, especially when your hands are filled with tools or materials. Because an occupancy sensor will turn off the lights when it doesn't detect movement, it can occasionally leave you in the dark.

Zoning saves energy. A simple but effective setup is to have one zone for your bench or finishing table and another for the machine area.

Attach a mounting block to your bench. Many desk lights have a post that can fit into a block screwed to your bench for easy installation and removal.

Task lighting. With most of the light provided by overhead fluorescents, task lighting is about filling the gaps.

Tall machines cast a shadow. Bandsaws and drill presses, with their large cabinets and motor housings, often block overhead lighting, but the fix is easy: a magnetic-base task light aimed right at the work.

Raking light reveals surface flaws.
Inexpensive stand-mounted halogen work lights
are a great way to provide low-angle light for
surface prep and finishing (above). The raking
light can highlight machine marks that are
invisible under overhead light (right).

Task lighting

Overhead fluorescents are good for general
ambient light, but for finishing and bench
work, you'll need additional task lighting.
Swing-arm lamps like those found on
drafting tables are great for aiming light
directly where you need it. Twin-head
halogen work lights are great for finishing

because they can provide raking light that
makes it easier to see runs and other problems.

Having a well-lit shop is a lot like having
a well-heated one. The shop becomes a more
welcoming place, a playground for your
creativity.

Treat Your Feet

STEVE SCOTT

Any woodworker who spends long afternoons on a concrete floor in the basement or garage knows there is a physical price to pay for enjoying one's hobby. Research confirms that standing on a hard floor for hours at a time will leave you with achy feet, legs, and back. Concrete is a punishing surface.

The solution is to put something more forgiving between your feet and the concrete. But what if you don't want or can't afford a whole new shop floor? The common answer for most people is anti-fatigue mats, those rubbery slabs that go underfoot where you spend the most time standing. With a little digging, I uncovered a wide range of choices. But before whipping out the company credit card, I did a bit of research to see what the experts say.

They really do work

There are no standards—industry, government, or otherwise—for what constitutes an "anti-fatigue" floor mat. In general, they are made of rubber or closed-cell foam and they range from ⅜ in. to 1 in. thick. But studies show that these mats do prevent pain in the feet and legs. One recent study at the University of Pittsburgh concluded that anti-fatigue mats made a significant difference, and especially so when the test subjects stood for more than two hours.

Protection. An anti-fatigue mat's cushioning helps prevent serious damage to chisel edges, squares, and other tools.

Insulation. Cold floor, warm feet. A mat is a barrier between your feet and a chilly concrete slab.

Comfort. Anti-fatigue mats offer a range of benefits. Mainly, they help cushion your feet and prevent pain and aches. Some say they do this by encouraging subtle movements of your feet and legs that improve circulation.

Rubber. Solid rubber mats are extremely durable, but most don't provide as soft a cushion as foam.

Foam. A good foam mat has a little more "give" than solid rubber but enough resilience to prevent pain and fatigue.

Exactly how they work is a bit of a mystery, however. Apart from providing a simple cushion between foot and floor, one theory holds that the mat's resilience encourages subtle movements of the feet and legs that help promote circulation. This keeps the blood from settling uncomfortably in your lower limbs.

In any case, anti-fatigue mats have become a staple of workplace design, said Tom Waters, a senior safety engineer at the National Institute of Occupational Safety and Health. The mats are recommended for grocery checkers, assembly-line workers, kitchen staff, operating-room nurses—just about anyone who spends most of the workday standing in one place.

Woodworkers swear by them, too. Marc Adams spent nearly $4,000 to put mats on the concrete floor at each of his school's 65 student benches. He credits the mats—made of ½-in.-thick foam—with making a full day at the bench much less taxing.

Deneb Puchalski considers a mat essential for the hand-tool demonstrations he does for Lie-Nielsen Toolworks®. The demos typically take place in convention spaces with concrete

Foam at heart. The rubber covering is durable and creates a nicely beveled edge.

Soft shell. A soft vinyl cover keeps the foam free of dust and safe from abrasion by shoe treads. It should be fine for most shops.

Hard shell. A layer of rubber or flexible plastic about ⅛ in. thick gives the foam better protection against sharp edges and abrasion.

floors. Before he began using the mats, he said, "my feet and legs would be a mess."

What to look for

Once I found out that mats really work, the next step was to find out whether some work better than others. They do. The good news is that a ½-in. foam mat will probably work just fine for you. Here's what to look for.

Material

Mats are most often made either from solid rubber or from closed-cell foam. For the home shop, foam is best. Solid rubber offers terrific durability but is quite firm underfoot and heavier than foam. These attributes are great for constant use in an industrial setting, but less crucial in a garage or basement.

A foam mat provides a better balance of support and cushioning for less-intensive use.

Covering

The sponge at the heart of most foam mats wouldn't stand up long to abrasion caused by shoes, dust, sharp chips, and tool edges. For this reason, the sponge is typically bonded to an outer skin of textured vinyl. Marc Adams reports that the vinyl-covered mats in his school have stood up to more than four years of heavy use with no serious damage. Still, for greater protection, some manufacturers offer mats with an armor-like layer of rubber or semi-rigid plastic. These are pricier but easier to sweep off.

TOO THIN

Not enough cushion. At ¼ in. thick, this yoga mat doesn't put enough foam between you and the concrete.

Just right. Mark Redfern, an ergonomics researcher, suggests a mat that's about ½ in. thick and relatively firm.

TOO THICK

Overkill. An extra-beefy mat like this 1-in.-thick model isn't dramatically more comfortable than a ½-in. or ⅝-in. mat. But it will make your footing less stable.

One for the bench. A long mat like this one offers support for tasks like planing long stock that require the full length of the bench.

And one for the tablesaw. This 2x3 mat offers plenty of standing surface for stationary tasks like cutting joinery or trimming parts to final size.

Thickness

Mark Redfern, an ergonomics researcher who authored the Pittsburgh study, suggests looking for a foam mat that's ½ in. thick or so and relatively firm. A mat that's too thin or soft will bottom out, compressing so much that your foot is basically resting on concrete again. A mat that's too thick and soft, he suggests, can make for unsteady footing. Regardless of thickness, experts agree that it's worth looking for a mat with gently beveled edges, which are less likely to catch a toe and send you sprawling.

What size and where to put them

The cost-conscious among us may be drawn to a small mat, and that is fine. A well-made 2x3 mat—the smallest commonly available—will cushion your feet just as effectively as a larger one. But a larger mat offers much more maneuvering room. A 2x3 mat might be perfect at the drill press, but it's not the most adequate runway for the back-and-forth travel you'll do at your bench.

If you had enough money, you could put one of these mats at every workstation in the shop. But let's assume you're working on a budget and will be doing this one piece at a time. Consider the type of work you do and where you spend the most time in the shop. Here are our suggestions, in order of priority:

The bench—This is a natural starting place. Any work you'll do at the bench is typically slow-paced (fitting joinery, surfacing by hand, etc.) and requires a lot of time and attention. Because you'll move back and forth from front vise to end vise, a 2x5 or larger mat is a good size.

The tablesaw—The saw's versatility for both milling and joinery means it's in use nearly every time I visit the shop. But it's the joinery cuts—small scale and repetitive—that will have you standing at the saw for a long time. For those, a 2x3 mat fits the bill.

Other tools—Share a smaller mat, or place individual mats at the bandsaw, router table, chopsaw, and drill press.

Placing mats around the shop

A mat comes in handy anyplace in the shop where you stand still for extended periods of time while working. The top priorities are the bench and tablesaw, but you should also consider putting mats at the bandsaw, drill press, and certainly the lathe. They are less crucial at the jointer or planer, where you walk back and forth during use.

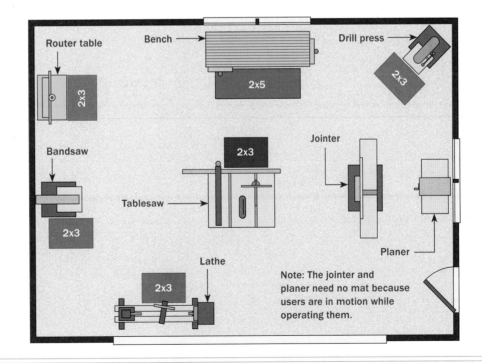

Note: The jointer and planer need no mat because users are in motion while operating them.

Low-Cost Shop Floor

SCOTT GIBSON

Many a shop is a converted two-car garage built on a concrete slab. I'll say this much for concrete: It's easy to sweep clean. It's also unforgiving. By mid-afternoon, feet hurt. By evening, a dull ache creeps up the back. Tools can be damaged if they're dropped on concrete. And in cold climates, concrete can be a heat sink.

One solution is to install a wood floor directly over the concrete. A wood surface is easier on your feet as well as any tools that roll off the bench. There are other advantages. Electric cable can be routed beneath the floor to power equipment located away from walls. Stationary tools, workbenches, and other fixtures can be screwed down easily. If there is enough headroom, a wood floor can be raised enough to locate dust-collection ducts below. And the cost of material for covering a concrete floor with wood is minimal.

However, if a wood floor is going to drop the ceiling height to less than 8 ft., I'd think twice about adding one. But a floor consisting of 2x4 sleepers and ¾-in.-thick plywood is only 2¼ in. thick.

Lay out the sleepers first

Because the sleepers will be in direct contact with concrete (for a permanent floor), they should be pressure-treated material rated for ground contact. Concrete can absorb water

Plywood floor over concrete slab

For a permanent floor, attach 2x4s to the concrete slab using construction adhesive and powder-actuated nails.

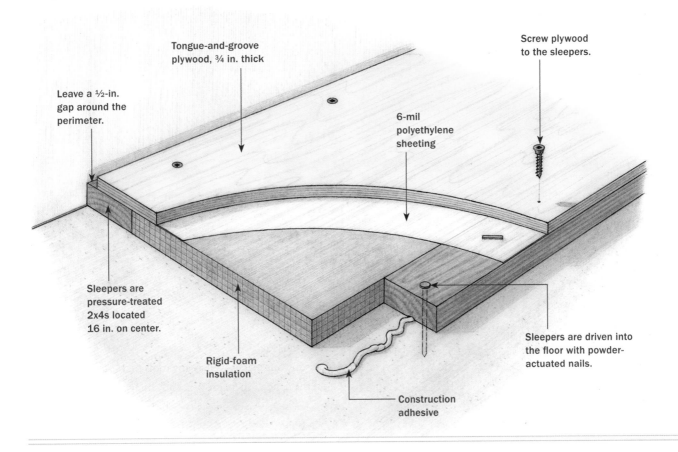

Leave a ½-in. gap around the perimeter.

Tongue-and-groove plywood, ¾ in. thick

Screw plywood to the sleepers.

6-mil polyethylene sheeting

Sleepers are pressure-treated 2x4s located 16 in. on center.

Rigid-foam insulation

Construction adhesive

Sleepers are driven into the floor with powder-actuated nails.

Temporary floor

For a removable floor, leave out the adhesive and fasteners, and place the polyethylene sheeting directly on the concrete. To keep the floor from lifting should it warp, attach a base molding around the perimeter walls.

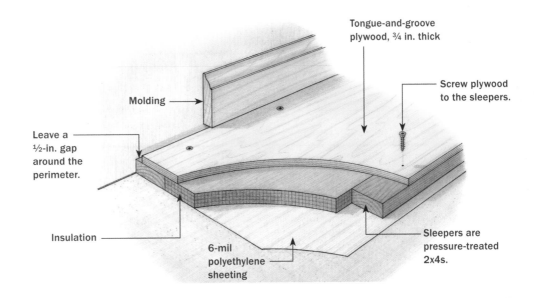

Molding

Leave a ½-in. gap around the perimeter.

Tongue-and-groove plywood, ¾ in. thick

Screw plywood to the sleepers.

Insulation

6-mil polyethylene sheeting

Sleepers are pressure-treated 2x4s.

Glue and nail the sleepers. Construction adhesive and nails provide added holding power. Lay a bead of glue under each sleeper, then nail it to the concrete using a powder-actuated driver.

like a sponge, and untreated wood not only decays, but it also invites carpenter ants and termites.

Don't forget to wear eye and lung protection when cutting pressure-treated wood and to wear gloves when handling it (splinters are nasty). Even though damp concrete won't degrade pressure-treated material for a very long time, really serious water problems should be cured before the new floor goes down. In a basement shop, that may mean cutting a trench at the perimeter of the room and installing a subsurface drain system and sump pump. Better to do that now.

Sleepers are laid flat, not on edge, over the concrete. They should be spaced 16 in. on

Concrete: The floor of hard knocks

Industrial ergonomists—specialists who look for ways to make the workplace more user-friendly— would rather see you work on almost any surface other than plain concrete.

"Concrete floors are a very hard, very dense material. As a result, if you have to stand on them for any length of time, most likely you're going to experience some level of discomfort," said Rob Nerhood, director of consultative services for the NC Ergonomics Resource Center in Raleigh, N.C.

Dan MacLeod, a consultant in ergonomics in Milford, Pa., said standing on hard surfaces can result in a variety of ailments, including fatigue, stress on the spinal column and heel spurs. "The latter is more or less a type of tendinitis of the heel," he said, "the symptoms for which are sore heels, particularly in the morning when you first get out of bed."

Adding a floor of 2x4 sleepers and plywood over a concrete slab does provide some relief. But consider also using anti-fatigue mats. Nerhood said the goal is to provide a material that can be compressed, even slightly, as a buffer between a worker's feet and a hard floor.

Don't overlook your work shoes, either. Insoles can wear out long before the outside of a shoe shows much wear and tear. "If you can't improve the floor," Nerhood said, "improving where your body interacts with the floor at the feet is one of the good steps you can take." No pun intended.

The cure for sore feet.
A comfortable pair of shoes and anti-fatigue mats will increase your comfort level on any type of floor.

center so that the long edges of the plywood always fall on solid wood (see drawings on p. 69). An easy way to get the layout right is to snap chalklines on the concrete to mark the edge of each 2x4. Snap the first line 14¾ in. from the wall, then add 16 in. to each successive line. Sleepers will span minor gaps and voids in the concrete, but serious dips should be filled before installing the

floor. Be sure to use a cold chisel to knock off any obstructions that would prevent the sleepers from lying flat.

Once all of the sleepers have been cut to size, place them on or near the layout lines. Then, starting at one end of the room, pick up a sleeper and lay a fat bead of construction adhesive on the floor where the center of the sleeper will fall. Press the sleeper into place.

Insulation to keep your toes warm. In colder climates, place rigid insulation between the rows of sleepers.

Sheeting provides a vapor barrier. Spread 6-mil polyethylene sheeting across the top of the sleepers and insulation. Cover the whole space, and if you need more than one sheet, overlap seams by 6 in.

Get the first piece right. Take your time placing the first plywood sheet because all of the other pieces will follow its course. Be sure to leave a ½-in. gap at the walls around the perimeter to give the plywood some room to expand.

Adhesive alone should hold down the 2x4s, but I recommend using powder-actuated nails, which will ensure that the wood is secure. Powder-actuated nails are inexpensive, and you can find them at a local hardware store. Don't, however, skip the adhesive and rely on powder-actuated fasteners alone. Over time, the floor can wiggle loose. Because the adhesive starts to dry quickly, glue down one sleeper at a time. Remember to leave a ½-in. gap between the walls and perimeter sleepers. In a cold climate, a layer of rigid-foam insulation cut to fit snugly between the 2x4s helps keep out the chill.

Follow with plastic sheeting and plywood

Once the 2x4s have been anchored to the floor, they should be covered with a layer of 6-mil polyethylene sheeting. The sheeting prevents moisture from migrating up through the floor and protects the plywood from damp air. Overlap any seams by 6 in. and tape them with housewrap tape. If the floor is not to be permanent, omit the adhesive and fasteners and allow the sleepers to float on the concrete. Lay the polyethylene directly over the concrete first, then lay the sleepers on top of the polyethylene (see drawing on p. 69).

Plywood is next. My first choice would be ¾-in.-thick tongue-and-groove, exterior-grade plywood, but you also can use oriented-strand board (OSB), which is less expensive. Arrange the sheets so that the seams are staggered. That is, start in one corner with a half sheet. On the next course, start with a full sheet. That way, the seams will be staggered 4 ft. apart. The plywood can be nailed to the sleepers, but screws allow you to remove and replace damaged plywood sheets easily. Fasten the plywood every 16 in. with either steel wood screws or drywall screws.

Although plywood is more dimensionally stable than solid wood, it's not a good idea to run the edge of the sheets right up to the wall. Leave a gap of ½ in. all the way around to give the plywood a little breathing room. You can cover the gap with a piece of baseboard or shoe molding.

Finishing the floor is a matter of personal preference. A coat or two of paint or clear finish will help protect the plywood from the inevitable coffee or paint spill. But for a shop, that may be more trouble than it's worth. Your feet, knees, ankles, and back—as well as your edge tools—will be just as happy with an unfinished floor.

A Revolution in Dust Collection

ASA CHRISTIANA

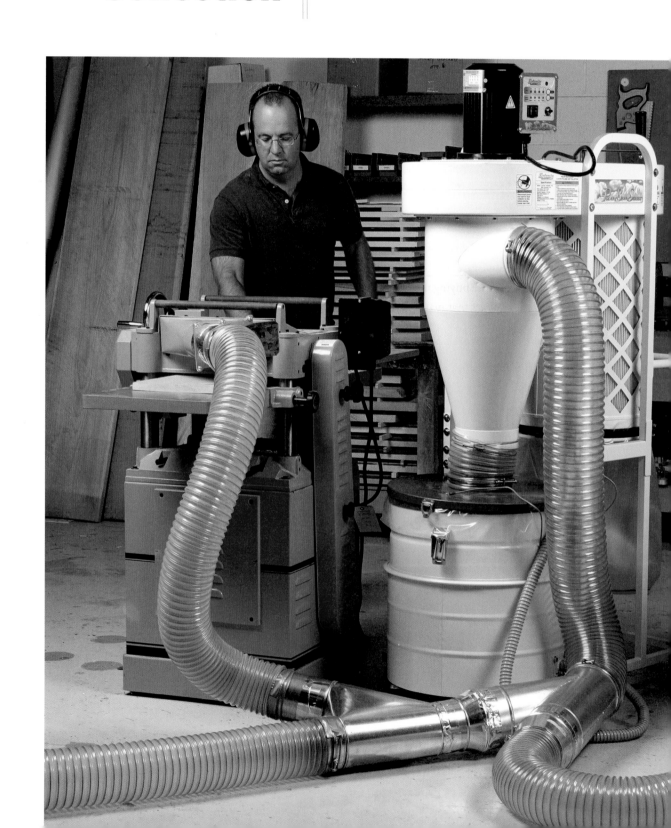

In 2002, wood dust went from being a nuisance to an official health risk. That's when the U.S. government put it on its list of "known carcinogens," linking it to a variety of nose, throat, and lung cancers. But it has taken our corner of the woodworking industry a while to catch up with reality.

The best way to manage dust is to collect it at the source, and one of the industry's first important realizations was that the dust ports were sadly lacking on most woodworking tools and nonexistent on others. That was pretty easy to fix, and the improvements have been steady and significant. So before you spend money on ceiling-hung air filters or expensive respirators, go to the source of the problem. Connect your dust collector and shop vacuum to every possible power tool. If you are buying new tools, look for manufacturers that make dust collection convenient and effective. For your existing tools, take a day in the shop to improve the ports.

The filtration story

Fifteen or 20 years ago, if you collected dust at all, you probably did it with a single-stage collector and a 30-micron polyester bag. Those porous bags act like fine-dust delivery systems, blasting out a cloud of the most dangerous stuff at head height. The irony is that people who didn't bother with dust collection at all, leaving big piles of sawdust under their tablesaws, were probably safer!

The trouble with wood dust is that the most dangerous particles, the very fine ones, are the hardest to collect. Under 10 microns in size, they hang longest in the air, penetrate deepest into the lungs, and are the hardest for the body to eject.

Small cyclones, tiny cyclones. One of the breakthroughs in dust collection involves downsizing. There is no doubt that the cyclone is the best way to collect dust. New portable models (see the facing page) are a more affordable option for small shops, while even smaller versions work wonders as dust separators for shop vacuums (above) and single-stage dust collectors.

Why two stages are better than one

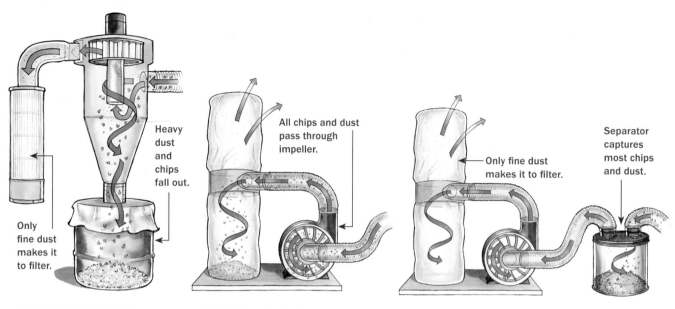

Heavy dust and chips fall out.

Only fine dust makes it to filter.

All chips and dust pass through impeller.

Only fine dust makes it to filter.

Separator captures most chips and dust.

THE CYCLONE IS KING

A cyclone has two stages. Dust is drawn first into the cyclone itself. All but the very finest particles fly to the outside of the cone and spiral down into a collecting bucket, leaving mostly clean air to be drawn up through the center of the funnel cloud and into the filter stage.

MOST COLLECTORS AND VACS ARE SINGLE-STAGE

Single-stage dust collectors (and most shop vacuums) draw air and chips directly into the collection area, where they clog filters, choking airflow and reducing suction.

ADD A SEPARATOR TO CREATE A TWO-STAGE SYSTEM

A dust separator turns a single-stage collector (or vac) into a two-stage system, grabbing the vast majority of the dust before it reaches the filter, keeping it clean and effective.

So the tool companies knew they had to get serious about filtration. Felt bags were an early response, borrowed from industry. But the finer the felt, the taller the bag needed to be in order to have enough surface area for good airflow. There's room for that in a factory but not a small shop. Enter the pleated filter, which packs hundreds of square feet of surface area into a small canister. You see these now on the latest cyclones, single-stage dust collectors, and shop vacuums, and they certainly are a major upgrade from the filters of the past. But for everything but the cyclones, there is a problem: The filters can only get so fine before they start clogging and killing airflow.

Why the cyclone is still best—Filters work best on two-stage collectors (like cyclones). A two-stage system catches most of the dust before it can get to the filter. That means the filter can be much finer.

On single-stage dust collectors (and most shop vacuums), most of the fine dust reaches the filter, so the very finest pleated filters will quickly pack with dust and start killing suction. At least five manufacturers of single-stage dust collectors told me the same thing: that they had to stop at 2-micron pleated filters when outfitting those machines. On the other hand, cyclone collectors can have state-of-the-art filters that capture particles as small as 0.3 microns. (For the bottom line

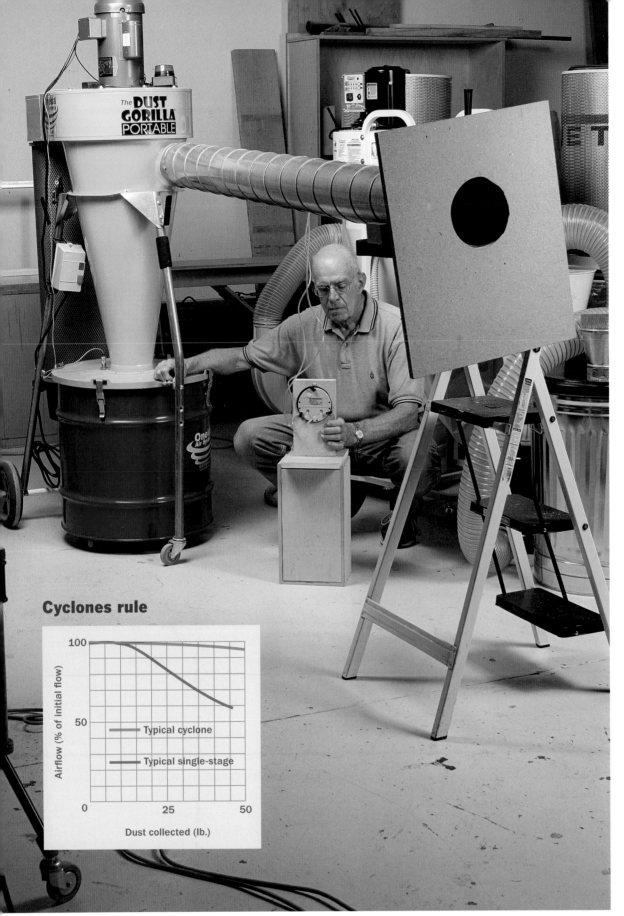

Cyclones rule

Airflow (% of initial flow)

100

50

—— Typical cyclone

—— Typical single-stage

0   25   50

Dust collected (lb.)

Single-stagers need help

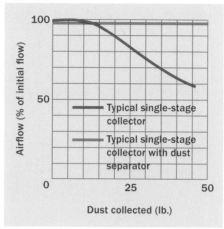

A separator makes a dramatic improvement. Although it sapped a bit of the initial airflow, the Oneida Super Dust Deputy removed 99% of the dust before it reached the filter of this JET Tools dust collector, keeping the airflow steady. Frequent filter cleaning was also effective.

on filter ratings, see "The truth about filtration" on p. 84.)

So my first piece of advice is to buy a cyclone dust collector if you can. While the first cyclones for small shops were big, expensive, stationary machines, requiring long hose or rigid-duct runs to reach all four corners of a shop, almost every cyclone manufacturer now makes compact, roll-around models.

Separators for the rest of us

I would love to trade up for a cyclone collector, but I recently exhausted my marital capital on a bigger bandsaw and a planer/jointer with a segmented cutterhead. So I have the same setup you probably have: a single-stage collector and a shop vacuum.

I've done my best to upgrade them. I put a "2-micron" cartridge filter on my dust collector and replaced the standard filter on my

WITHOUT SEPARATOR

Same cure for shop vacs. We outfitted shop vacuums with HEPA filters, and tested them with and without separators. The difference was undeniable, both in airflow and filter condition. The only vac that maintained its suction without a separator was the Bosch Airsweep™.

Separators super-charge shop vacuums

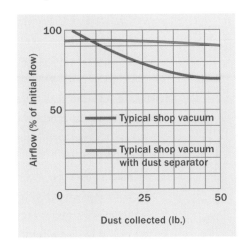

Airflow (% of initial flow)

100

50

0   25   50

Dust collected (lb.)

— Typical shop vacuum

— Typical shop vacuum with dust separator

WITH SEPARATOR

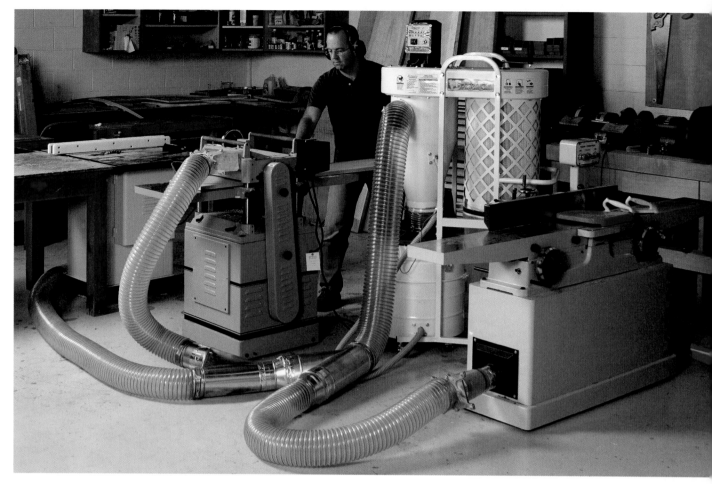

Find a cyclone with a fine filter. Grizzly, Oneida, and Penn State are three companies whose cyclone filters are rated MERV 15 or higher (see "The truth about filtration" on p. 84). Or upgrade the cyclone you have. Grizzly, Oneida, and Penn State also sell their filters as accessories.

vac with a HEPA model (the finest filtration available). But the HEPA filter came with a cost: I have to bang it against my trash can regularly to unclog it and restore the vacuum's suction. That's not only a pain, but it also fills my head with the same fine dust I'm trying to avoid. And I've known for some time that the 2-micron filter on my collector was not up to snuff.

The light went on for me when I recently reviewed the new Dust Deputy from Oneida. It is a small plastic cyclone separator for shop vacuums, and I was astounded at how clean it kept my HEPA filter and how much more powerful the airflow was as a result.

Dust separators are nothing new, and they are made for both shop vacuums and single-stage dust collectors. The common type is not much more than an inlet and outlet that attach to the top of a barrel. Dust reaches the barrel first, where the larger particles spin around and settle out before the air passes out of the barrel and into the dust collector itself. Oneida's little cyclone is just a new type of separator.

My experience with the Dust Deputy got me thinking: Could I upgrade the cartridge filter on my single-stage dust collector and then install a separator to keep that filter from clogging constantly? Or do I have to spring for a cyclone to be truly safe?

Testing, testing

To answer these questions and more, I started researching this article. I spoke with product managers from eight companies; brought in the best cyclones, single-stagers, shop vacuums, aftermarket filters, and dust separators for testing; and enlisted the help of *Fine Woodworking* shop manager Bill Peck, a retired engineer. He dug our pitot tube and digital manometer (devices for measuring airflow) out of storage, and borrowed bags of dust from a local shop.

No surprise: Cyclones rule—First, Peck measured the initial airflow on every dust collector and vacuum to get a baseline for each with a clean filter. Then he turned them on and sucked up enough dust to fill each one to capacity, measuring flow the whole time. That told us that the experts are right about cyclones: They work better than any other type of collector. While the airflow/suction on the other dust collectors and vacs dipped up to 40 percent as their filters clogged, the filters on the cyclones stayed clean and the airflow barely wavered.

Better filters are on the way

As a result of this article, both Grizzly and Oneida have agreed to make and sell upgraded filters for single-stage collectors, with the same filter material used in their cyclone filters. The Oneida FXK011820 HEPA and the Grizzly T23916 are available now.

How to test single-stagers?—After seeing what a dust separator did for my shop vacuum, allowing it to have a much finer filter without clogging, I couldn't wait to try out the separators made for single-stage dust collectors. That's when we hit a roadblock: No one makes an aftermarket filter for single-stage collectors that's any better than the standard-issue models. (But that's about to change. See "Better filters are on the way" above.)

So we couldn't upgrade the filters on the single-stage collectors, but we could do two things that would get us very close to a definitive answer. First, we could test the effect of a dust separator on a single-stage collector

Use a dust separator to keep the filter clean. This Veritas® Cyclone Lid is an affordable upgrade for any single-stage dust collector. Separators are also easier to empty than bags.

The standouts. Our favorite model was the Super Dust Deputy (www.oneida-Air.com), which captured 99% of the dust. But the Woodcraft® Trash Can Cyclone Lid (www.woodcraft.com) was our choice for best value with 90% of the dust captured.

Or clean the filter yourself—frequently. Spinning the internal flappers or blowing with compressed air will return the airflow to normal, but you must do it after each woodworking session.

with its standard pleated filter in place. If the separators worked well for those, they should help even finer filters too. Second, we could do the full test on our army of shop vacuums, since there are dust separators and upgraded filters available for all of those.

Separators work wonders on single-stage collectors—We started by testing a number of typical single-stage collectors, trying them without a separator in place, and the results were sobering: Airflow dropped by an average of 40% after filling the bags

Faithful companion. A dust separator tags along with your shop vacuum, capturing 99% of the dust before it can clog the filter.

Add a HEPA filter. Certified HEPA aftermarket filters are inexpensive and widely available for most shop vacuums. Go to www.cleanstream. com for more information. However, without a dust separator (left), a HEPA filter will clog more quickly than a standard one, reducing airflow significantly.

just once. One has to assume that number would be even higher with finer filters. Then we picked a typical performer, the Jet DC1100CK, and tried it with various dust separators. With the best separators, the airflow hardly budged! By the way, Jet makes a "Vortex" version of its single-stage collectors, and the one we tested recently kept its filter clean without the need for a separator.

We also tested the effectiveness of those internal flappers that manufacturers have in-cluded on their cartridge filters. They worked great, too. A few spins of the handles this way and that unpacked the pleats and brought the airflow back to normal. Blowing compressed air through the pleats also worked very well, and won't abrade the filter media the way flappers might. We also found that a full bag drives the dust swirl higher, clogging the filter more quickly, so we recommend emptying the bag when it is half full or so.

The truth about filtration

There is a lot of mystery and misinformation surrounding filtration specs, so I took a closer look. Manufacturers tend to give vague ratings like "2 micron." If a filter rating doesn't tell you what percentage of what size particles it can capture, the manufacturer probably doesn't know exactly. Although the science of filter ratings is new to our corner of the woodworking industry, there are plenty of independent companies in Europe and the United States that can test and rate filter media at very low cost, and a few manufacturers have taken advantage of that.

Ratings are standardized. The widely accepted standard in the United States comes from the American Society of Heating, Refrigerating, and Air-Conditioning Engineers (ASHRAE), and is expressed as a minimum efficiency reporting value (MERV) or as HEPA (high-efficiency particulate air), a rating that exceeds the MERV scale. True HEPA filters capture 99.97% of 0.3-micron particles, which is as small as wood dust gets. For shop-vacuum filters, buy a certified HEPA filter, not "HEPA-type" or anything vague-sounding. For all other dust collectors, look for a filter that is third-party-rated to capture more than 85% of the 0.3-micron to 1.0-micron particles (MERV 15 or higher).

"2-micron" doesn't cut it. Here's what happened when we sucked the finest diatomaceous earth (powder used to test filtration) into a typical single-stage dust collector with a typical pleated filter.

Separators are a must-have for shop vacuums—The next test was tougher. We put both standard and HEPA filters onto a number of shop vacuums, sucked up gallons of dust, and measured the flow. Sure enough, the HEPA filters clogged more rapidly than standard models, just as I experienced in my own shop. Then we attached the separators, and they did their magic once again, keeping the filters clean and flowing free.

By the way, our tests showed that adding a separator does steal a small amount of initial airflow, but that loss is vastly outweighed by their advantage once you start pouring dust into the system.

The bottom line for safe woodworking

If you want to be safe from fine wood dust and have a cleaner shop in general, you should focus on two things: bringing the proper amount of suction to the source and putting the finest filtration you can buy at the other end.

True HEPA. Look for "HEPA," not "HEPA-type" or anything else. This aftermarket shop-vacuum filter is from Gore® CleanStream®.

Media ID :   Oneida GE HEPA
Test Type :   Fractional Efficiency
Test Aerosol :   KCl, Neutralized

Velocity (fpm)	10.5
Δp (" H$_2$O)	0.794
Size Range (μm)	Fractional Efficiency (%)
0.3-0.5	99.977
0.5-0.7	99.992
0.7-1.0	99.993
1.0-2.0	99.999
2.0-3.0	100.000
3.0-5.0	100.000
>5.0	100.000

Everything else should be tested and certified. For cyclone and single-stage dust collectors, look for filters that have been tested by a reputable third party to capture at least 85% of the finest dust particles. Manufacturers can have their filters tested and post the results online. Above is part of Oneida's third-party test report.

Choose the right power plant—Your primary source of suction for woodworking machinery should be a dust collector, not a shop vacuum. That's because you need as much as 700 cubic feet per minute of airflow at the end of the hose for larger machines. But it is possible to overbuild your system. Too much air pressure is actually a bad thing, since it can force dust right through a fine filter. So unless you are installing a full-shop system, with a stationary collector and permanent duct runs to every corner, a 2-hp dust

collector (either cyclone or single-stage) with a 12-in. impeller is probably right for a basement or garage shop.

With anything smaller, and even for 2-hp collectors, I recommend keeping the biggest machines as close as possible to each other to keep hose runs shorter (long runs add friction and slow airflow).

Check your filters—If you can afford it, get one of the new compact cyclones, with a filter that has been rated by a reputable third party. We found three manufacturers with certified, state-of-the-art filters—Grizzly Industrial® Inc., Oneida, and Penn State Industries. And filters from those companies can be purchased as accessories and retrofit onto an existing cyclone. But other manufacturers are upgrading all the time, so check websites for current stats and testing info.

If a single-stage collector is a better fit for your budget, or if you already own one, consider the upgraded filters coming from Grizzly and Oneida. Most collectors have similar dimensions and designs, so there should be an aftermarket filter that will fit yours. After upgrading, consider adding a dust separator to keep the filter clean and the airflow powerful.

Of course, no matter what type of collector you get, you'll need a shop vacuum that can go where its big brother can't. Put a HEPA filter on yours, or buy a new one with HEPA standard. And unless your vac has some kind of self-cleaning feature (a few have built-in filter shakers), add a dust separator to keep that HEPA filter from clogging and killing airflow.

A Workbench 30 Years in the Making

GARRETT HACK

When I built my first bench well over 30 years ago, I had limited furniture-making experience, so I adapted the design from some benches I had used in various classes. That first bench has been a solid friend in the shop for many years. But as my experience level increased, I kept a mental list of improvements I'd make if I were to build a new one. I recently said as much in a lecture at Colonial Williamsburg, and *Fine Woodworking* decided to pay me to stop procrastinating.

Over the years, I've developed a love of hand tools. I use them in every aspect of furniture making, and details made with these elegant tools are a signature of my work. So my first priority was to make the new bench better suited to my hand-tool habits.

What makes a bench work

In building this bench, I wanted a tool that would withstand the daily stresses heaped upon it, and the materials and design reflect that approach. A bench can be fashioned with humble materials (any dense and stable hardwood will do) and basic joinery and work very well.

Add beef—The benchtop is big enough to clamp a large case piece in almost any arrangement, with room for many tools, and it's thick and sturdy. The base of the bench can hold a heavy load (the top weighs more than 200 lb.), but more importantly it's

Peg the short rails. The trestles are assembled with beefy mortise-and-tenons joints. The rails are reinforced with hardwood pegs.

Wedge the shoes. The mortises and tenons in the top and bottom of the trestles are wedged.

Big stretchers. Threaded rod gives a secure connection between the stretchers and trestles.

Anatomy of a great bench

To build this bench, you'll need lots of clamps and glue. The trickiest parts will be the top (p. 90), which is built up in layers to get the 3-in. thickness, and the tail-vise assembly (p. 94). On the other hand, the trestle base is assembled with straightforward mortise-and-tenon joinery.

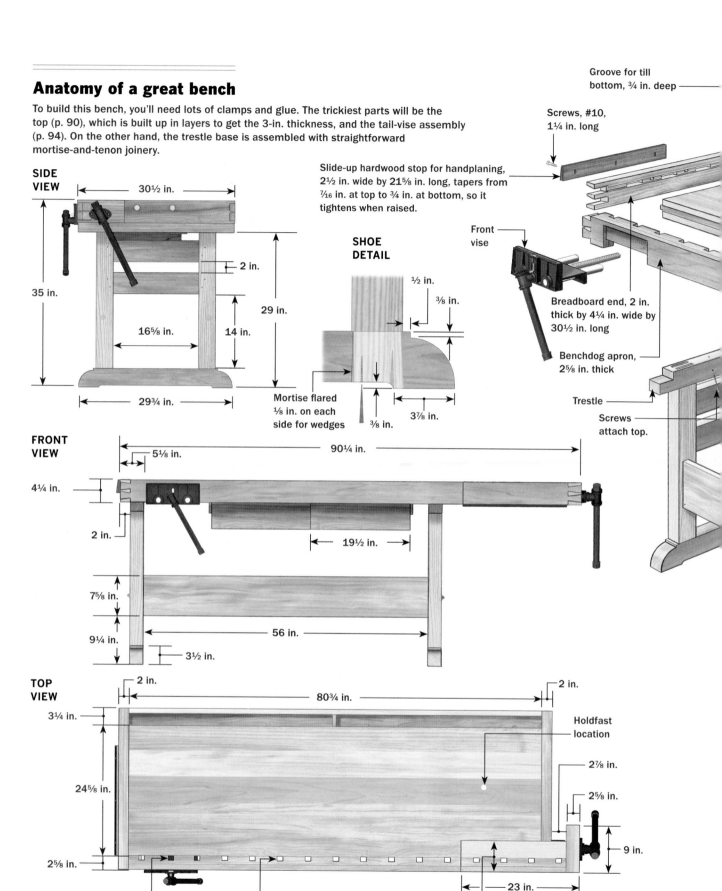

SIDE VIEW

30½ in.

35 in.

2 in.

29 in.

16⅝ in.

14 in.

29¾ in.

Slide-up hardwood stop for handplaning, 2½ in. wide by 21⅝ in. long, tapers from ⁷⁄₁₆ in. at top to ¾ in. at bottom, so it tightens when raised.

SHOE DETAIL

½ in.

⅜ in.

Mortise flared ⅛ in. on each side for wedges

⅜ in.

3⅞ in.

Groove for till bottom, ¾ in. deep

Screws, #10, 1¼ in. long

Front vise

Breadboard end, 2 in. thick by 4¼ in. wide by 30½ in. long

Benchdog apron, 2⅝ in. thick

Trestle

Screws attach top.

FRONT VIEW

5⅛ in.

90¼ in.

4¼ in.

2 in.

19½ in.

7⅝ in.

9¼ in.

56 in.

3½ in.

TOP VIEW

2 in.

80¾ in.

2 in.

3¼ in.

Holdfast location

24⅝ in.

2⅞ in.

2⅝ in.

9 in.

2⅝ in.

23 in.

5⅝ in.

Align this dog hole with dog in vise.

Dog holes, ⅞ in. wide by 1⅛ in. long, spaced roughly 5 in. on center

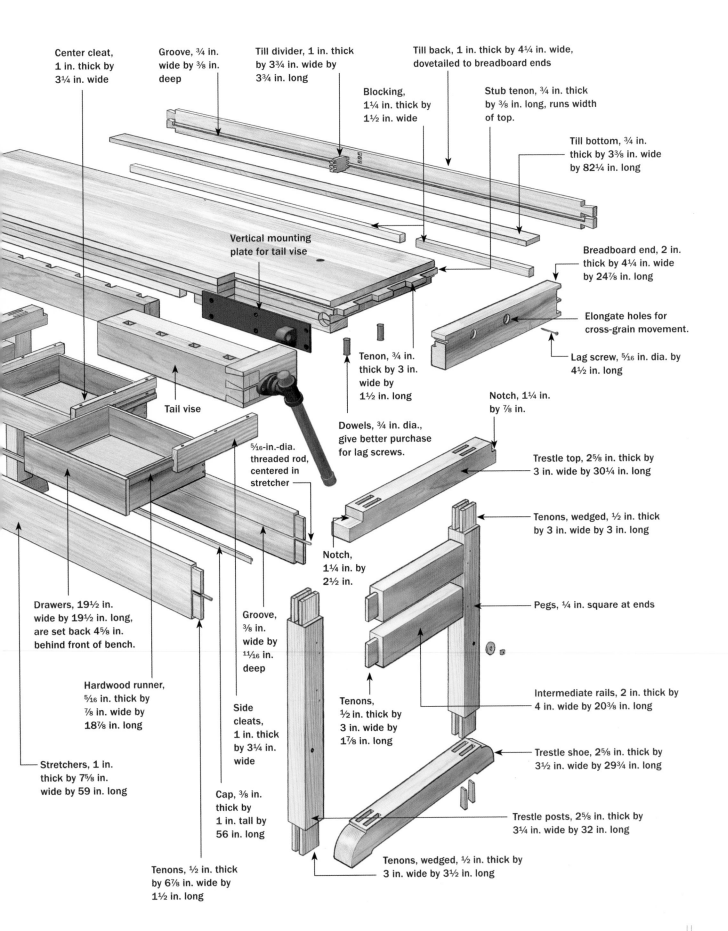

Center cleat, 1 in. thick by 3¼ in. wide

Groove, ¾ in. wide by ⅜ in. deep

Till divider, 1 in. thick by 3¾ in. wide by 3¾ in. long

Till back, 1 in. thick by 4¼ in. wide, dovetailed to breadboard ends

Blocking, 1¼ in. thick by 1½ in. wide

Stub tenon, ¾ in. thick by ⅜ in. long, runs width of top.

Till bottom, ¾ in. thick by 3⅜ in. wide by 82¼ in. long

Vertical mounting plate for tail vise

Breadboard end, 2 in. thick by 4¼ in. wide by 24⅞ in. long

Elongate holes for cross-grain movement.

Tail vise

Tenon, ¾ in. thick by 3 in. wide by 1½ in. long

Lag screw, ⁵⁄₁₆ in. dia. by 4½ in. long

Notch, 1¼ in. by ⅞ in.

⁵⁄₁₆-in.-dia. threaded rod, centered in stretcher

Dowels, ¾ in. dia., give better purchase for lag screws.

Trestle top, 2⅝ in. thick by 3 in. wide by 30¼ in. long

Tenons, wedged, ½ in. thick by 3 in. wide by 3 in. long

Notch, 1¼ in. by 2½ in.

Pegs, ¼ in. square at ends

Drawers, 19½ in. wide by 19½ in. long, are set back 4⅝ in. behind front of bench.

Groove, ⅜ in. wide by ¹¹⁄₁₆ in. deep

Tenons, ½ in. thick by 3 in. wide by 1⅞ in. long

Intermediate rails, 2 in. thick by 4 in. wide by 20⅜ in. long

Hardwood runner, ⁵⁄₁₆ in. thick by ⅞ in. wide by 18⅞ in. long

Side cleats, 1 in. thick by 3¼ in. wide

Trestle shoe, 2⅝ in. thick by 3½ in. wide by 29¾ in. long

Stretchers, 1 in. thick by 7⅝ in. wide by 59 in. long

Cap, ⅜ in. thick by 1 in. tall by 56 in. long

Trestle posts, 2⅝ in. thick by 3¼ in. wide by 32 in. long

Tenons, ½ in. thick by 6⅞ in. wide by 1½ in. long

Tenons, wedged, ½ in. thick by 3 in. wide by 3½ in. long

rigid enough to withstand the racking forces created by handplaning.

At 35 in. tall, my bench will work for a wide range of tasks, from handwork to machine work to assembly jobs. But I'm over 6 ft. tall. You may have to experiment to find a comfortable height.

Lots of ways to hold work—Because I do a lot of handwork, I need surefire ways to hold workpieces. In my experience, the best tools for the job are a front vise and a tail vise, used in tandem with benchdogs and a holdfast. Finally, I added a sliding stop at the left end. It can be set high or low and is useful for planing panels, thin drawer bottoms, table-tops, or multiple parts.

Tackle top in sections

Assemble the benchtop in sections on a pair of sturdy sawhorses. Offset the pieces in each section to create a strong tongue-and-groove interlock and guarantee alignment.

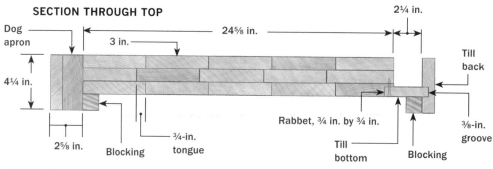

SECTION THROUGH TOP

Dog apron — 2¼ in. — 24⅝ in. — Till back — 4¼ in. — 3 in. — Rabbet, ¾ in. by ¾ in. — ⅜-in. groove — 2⅝ in. — Blocking — ¾-in. tongue — Till bottom — Blocking

Tongue-and-groove trick. First section kicks it off. Glue the first three boards together, then let the assembly dry. Clean up squeeze-out so it won't interfere with the following section.

Three boards at a time. After the glue dries from each previous section, add the next three boards, applying glue to all mating surfaces. Clamp across the faces and edges. Repeat until the whole slab of the top is assembled. You'll need lots of clamps. Use cauls to keep the assembly flat.

Build the top on a pair of strong horses

The top looks like a bunch of 12/4 planks glued together, but it's actually three layers of 1-in.-thick boards. This design is very stable so it will stay flat, and it's an economical way to use materials. I used hard maple, yellow birch, and beech, dedicating the best of the maple to the top layer and the breadboard ends, and using narrower and somewhat lower-quality material for the middle and bottom layers.

Glue up the top one section at a time. To make the job less stressful, I recommend Unibond 800, a slow-setting urea-formaldehyde glue (www.vacupress.com) typically used in vacuum veneering. Once you have the top glued together, use a circular saw to trim the benchtop to length. Clean up the edges with a scraper and a handplane, and flatten the top. When the top is flat, rout the rabbet for the till bottom on the back lower edge.

Make the benchdog apron—The benchdog apron is laminated from two pieces. After gluing the pieces together, lay out and cut the mortise for the front vise hardware in the apron; depending on the vise, you may need to cut a hollow under the top to accom-

modate the hardware. Once that's done, use a dado set to cut the dog holes. Attach the vise's rear jaw to the apron and then set the piece aside as you start working on the breadboard ends.

Breadboard ends are next—Cut the breadboard ends to width and thickness but leave them a bit long. Cut them to size after you lay out and cut the joinery to attach them to the benchtop. At the rear of each breadboard, rout the groove for the till bottom; it should align with the rabbet in the benchtop. Then drill holes for the lag screws that will help anchor the breadboards to the top. Finally, lay out and cut the dovetails.

Breadboards keep it flat.
After mortising the breadboard pieces, cut the tongue and tenons on the top. Use a router and fence to make the cheek cuts and a handsaw to remove the waste between the long tenons. Clean out the corners with chisels.

The apron frames the top. To allow for wood movement, the breadboard ends are tenoned to the top, with lag screws cinching the parts. Use slow-setting urea-formaldehyde glue everywhere else to buy time for fine-tuning.

Start at the front left corner. Connect the breadboard to the apron (left). Then apply glue to the breadboard tenons and to the interior face of the apron. Go lightly to avoid squeeze-out into the dog holes. Clamp the breadboard in place to help support the long dog apron (below left), then drive in the lags. The right-hand corner of the top (reversed in below right) will be notched for the tail vise, so there's no need to make the dog apron the full length of the bench.

The till goes on last. Screw the till bottom into its rabbet under the top. Glue the divider in the till back, then glue the assembly to the breadboard ends and the top.

Use a router and fence to cut the tenon cheeks on the ends of the top. Then lay out and cut the long tenons that will go deep into the breadboards. Clean up the inside corners with a chisel, and fine-tune the fit using handplanes.

Once the breadboards have been fitted, drill the pilot holes for the lag screws. To give the screws extra purchase (so they don't just go into weak end grain), I mortised hardwood dowels from under the benchtop, in line with the pilot holes.

Attach the breadboards, apron, and till—Start by gluing the apron to its breadboard end. Then apply glue to the apron and front edge of the benchtop. Screw on the breadboard end, and clamp the apron in place, working from the corner out. Don't worry about exactly where the apron ends; you'll be notching out that end of the benchtop for the tail vise. Finally, install the other breadboard end.

After the glue cures on the breadboard ends and the benchdog apron, install the till parts and 1x blocking underneath, which increases stiffness and gives better clamp purchase.

Assemble the base—Once the top has been glued together, build the trestles and make the stretchers of the base. Before gluing

Tail vise is a worthwhile challenge

Hack begins by notching out the front right corner of the benchtop. The vise design uses readily available steel hardware for the mechanical parts, housed in a shopmade wooden sliding jaw.

CROSS-SECTION

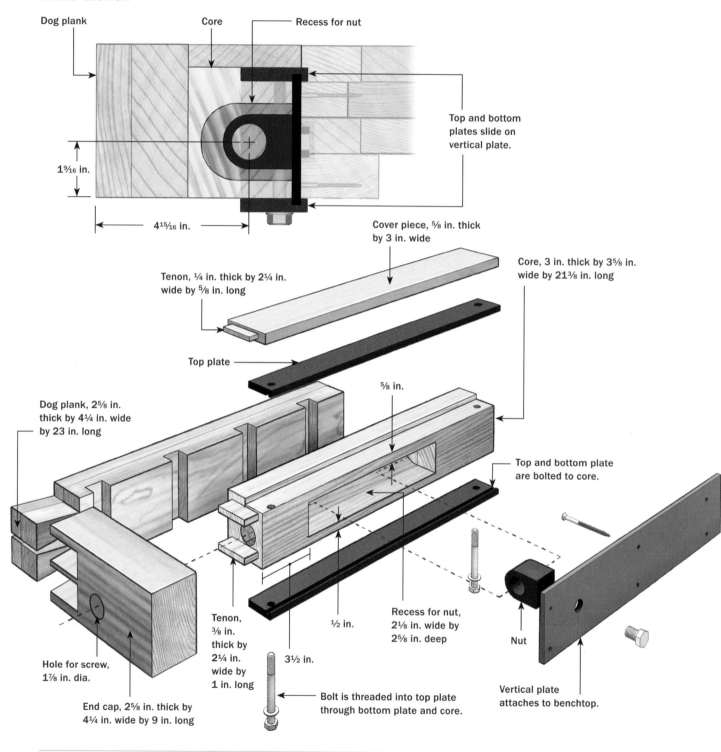

Dog plank

Core

Recess for nut

Top and bottom plates slide on vertical plate.

$1\frac{9}{16}$ in.

$4\frac{15}{16}$ in.

Tenon, $\frac{1}{4}$ in. thick by $2\frac{1}{4}$ in. wide by $\frac{5}{8}$ in. long

Cover piece, $\frac{5}{8}$ in. thick by 3 in. wide

Core, 3 in. thick by $3\frac{5}{8}$ in. wide by $21\frac{3}{8}$ in. long

Top plate

$\frac{5}{8}$ in.

Dog plank, $2\frac{5}{8}$ in. thick by $4\frac{1}{4}$ in. wide by 23 in. long

Top and bottom plate are bolted to core.

Recess for nut, $2\frac{1}{8}$ in. wide by $2\frac{5}{8}$ in. deep

Nut

Hole for screw, $1\frac{7}{8}$ in. dia.

Tenon, $\frac{3}{8}$ in. thick by $2\frac{1}{4}$ in. wide by 1 in. long

$\frac{1}{2}$ in.

$3\frac{1}{2}$ in.

End cap, $2\frac{5}{8}$ in. thick by $4\frac{1}{4}$ in. wide by 9 in. long

Bolt is threaded into top plate through bottom plate and core.

Vertical plate attaches to benchtop.

Make way for the top plate.
Use a three-wing slot cutter to rout a groove parallel to the benchtop to house the top plate. The vertical board tacked in the corner acts as a spacer to prevent the bit from cutting too far.

Attach the vertical plate.
Clamp the bottom plate in place. Align the top of the vertical plate with the groove, drill pilot holes, and drive in the top screws. Now attach the top and bottom plates and try the sliding action.

and wedging the top of the trestles, notch both ends to go around the benchdog apron in front and the till in back.

Add the tail vise

Building a smooth-working tail vise can take nearly as long as building the benchtop or base. The work is worthwhile because a tail vise is unmatched at holding work flat on the benchtop between dogs. Have the hardware in hand before you start, and make a full-scale drawing of the whole assembly

to make layout easier. Use a circular saw and hand tools to cut a notch in the benchtop for the vise, and tune the vertical surfaces square with the top. Rout the groove for the top plate (see top photo, above) a bit oversize to provide a little clearance and leave room for adjustment, if needed. Now attach the vertical mounting plate to the bench (with only two screws so you can adjust it later if need be), aligned with the top-plate slot and perfectly parallel with the benchtop.

Glue up the wood parts.
Dovetail the end cap to the dog
plank first. Next, remove the
top and bottom plates from the
core and glue it to the end cap
and to the dog plank. Try not to
get a lot of squeeze-out inside
the dog holes.

The core is key—The core of the vise
accommodates the screw and nut, and is laminated from two pieces. Before gluing them
together, hollow out the interior of one piece
with a core-box bit and router. The other
piece has a rectangular section removed with
a saw. Glue these two pieces together and let
them dry.

Now make the dog-hole plank and dovetail it to the end cap. Cut two mortises in the
end cap and mating tenons on the end of the
core, for alignment and added strength. Also,
cut the shallow mortise into the end cap and
a tenon on the end of the top cover. Cut a

shallow rabbet in the top edge for the top
guide plate.

Attach the top and bottom guide plates
to the core and slide it onto the plate on the
bench. Test the action—there should be little
wiggle when you lift the front edge, and the
core should move parallel to the bench. If the
guide plates grip the steel plate on the bench
too tightly, the core movement will be stiff.
Shim the bottom guide plate with a piece of
veneer or a business card. If you have lots of
wiggle, the plates need to be tighter together,
so deepen the rabbet for the top guide into
the core slightly and retest.

Mount the wood jaw to the hardware. Be sure to clean up the wood parts to remove any glue squeeze-out that could interfere with the assembly (left). Thread the bolts through the core, and then screw each plate to the core. Glue the top cover to the core and to the end cap (below).

Add the dog plank and top—When the core moves smoothly, remove it from the bench. Now glue the dog-hole plank and end cap together and to the core. Mount the assembly to the benchtop, adding the last screws to the mounting plate. Thread in the lead screw and fasten the flange to the end cap and test the vise action. Finally, install the top piece, which is tenoned into the end cap and glued to the top of the core.

Final details

Now finish the surface prep on the benchtop. Bring all surfaces flush and smooth using handplanes. I chamfered all edges with a block plane. Add the slide-up stop on the end of the bench, install the drawers, and make a couple of handles for your vises. Last, finish the top with two coats of boiled linseed oil.

The Wired Workbench

JOHN WHITE

In a modern shop, a lot of work gets done with power tools such as routers, biscuit joiners, and random-orbit sanders. But most of us use them on benches designed around handplaning, which means everything from the height to the mass to the vises and benchdogs is geared toward hand-tool use. So the editors at *Fine Woodworking* decided to build a bench designed for power tools. They posted a blog on www.FineWoodworking.com, asking readers what they thought a "wired workbench" should be. A lot of great suggestions came in, and being a veteran of the shop and an inveterate inventor, I was given the task of distilling readers' ideas into a user-friendly whole.

Power tools need electricity to run and they make dust by the fistful. So most people agreed that the first thing this bench needed was a built-in source of electricity and dust collection. I kept things simple by attaching a commercially available automated vacuum outlet, the iVAC switch box, that turns on the dust collection when you power up the tool. And I made room in the base for both a shop vacuum and an Oneida Dust Deputy, a miniature cyclone that has proven its value trapping the fine dust (and all of the chips) before it gets to the vacuum and clogs the filter (see "A Revolution in Dust Collection," p. 74).

Collect the dust, forget the fuss

Imagine locking down your workpieces quickly and using your portable power tools without any dust or distractions.

SMART VALET FOR CORDS AND HOSES

A simple hanger system manages these necessary evils, so they don't drag and disrupt your work.

CLEVER CLAMPING IS BUILT IN

Pipe clamps apply the pressure, and low-profile dogs stay out of the way of your tools.

SHOP VACUUM AT THE READY

Put a small vacuum in the cabinet and leave it there, ready to work. That way, you won't forget to hook it up or be tempted to do without.

HIGHER THAN A HAND-TOOL BENCH

Traditional benches are lower, so you can bear down on your bench planes. But power-tool tasks like routing and sanding are better at belly height.

DUST EMPTIES EASILY

The Dust Deputy grabs 99% of the chips and dust, dropping them into a box that's easy to empty and keeping the vacuum filter clean.

ONBOARD POWER

Plug your power tools into an automated vacuum switch that turns on the vacuum when you turn on the tool. It also runs the vacuum for a few seconds after the tool powers off.

Build the base first

Rather than fill the interior with drawers, we designed it to hide and muffle a shop vacuum and hold a dust separator. Construction is simple and solid: ¾-in. plywood and drywall screws.

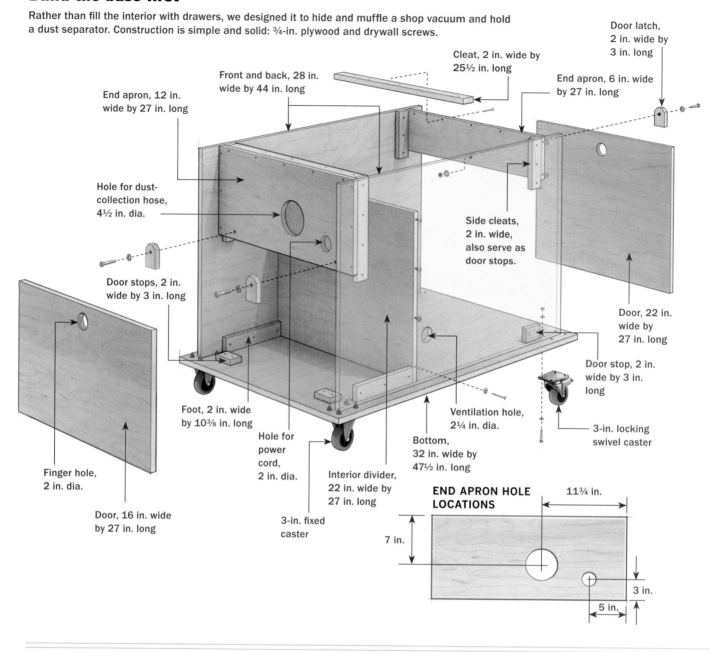

Door latch, 2 in. wide by 3 in. long

Cleat, 2 in. wide by 25½ in. long

End apron, 6 in. wide by 27 in. long

End apron, 12 in. wide by 27 in. long

Front and back, 28 in. wide by 44 in. long

Hole for dust-collection hose, 4½ in. dia.

Side cleats, 2 in. wide, also serve as door stops.

Door stops, 2 in. wide by 3 in. long

Door, 22 in. wide by 27 in. long

Door stop, 2 in. wide by 3 in. long

3-in. locking swivel caster

Finger hole, 2 in. dia.

Foot, 2 in. wide by 10⅜ in. long

Hole for power cord, 2 in. dia.

Interior divider, 22 in. wide by 27 in. long

Ventilation hole, 2¼ in. dia.

Bottom, 32 in. wide by 47½ in. long

3-in. fixed caster

Door, 16 in. wide by 27 in. long

END APRON HOLE LOCATIONS

11¾ in.

7 in.

3 in.

5 in.

This wired workbench also is taller (38 in. total) than traditional benches, moving the tool and the workpiece up to a height where you have better vision and control. It's wider, too, but not as long. I got rid of the traditional front and tail vises, opting for a simple but effective clamping system made from two pipe clamps. The benchdogs have soft heads that hold workpieces firmly, but won't dent or mar them. And there are locking casters underneath to make the bench mobile.

Finally, the wired workbench is much easier to make than a big, heavy traditional

Get a third hand for assembly. White used a simple plywood corner block to hold parts still and square to one another while he drove in screws.

Sources

DUST-DEPUTY MINIATURE CYCLONE

www.oneida-air.com
No. AXD001004
(90° elbow,
No. AHA000004)

IVAC SWITCH
www.ivacswitch.com

Add aprons for stiffness. Screw through the face into the cleats. On the cyclone end, predrill holes for the vacuum hose and power cords with a circle cutter.

bench. Because it won't take the forces a hand-tool bench does, the entire bench is made from plywood. And there is no complicated joinery, just butt joints held together by screws. Where they show, I've used stainless-steel deck screws and finish washers for a clean, modern look.

If you already have a heavy hand-tool workbench, this one will make a great, mobile, secondary workstation. And if you rely mostly on power tools, this might be the only bench you need.

Mini-cyclone drops dust into a bin

A mini-cyclone separates chips and dust out of the vacuum's airflow, dropping them into an easy-to-empty dust bin below.

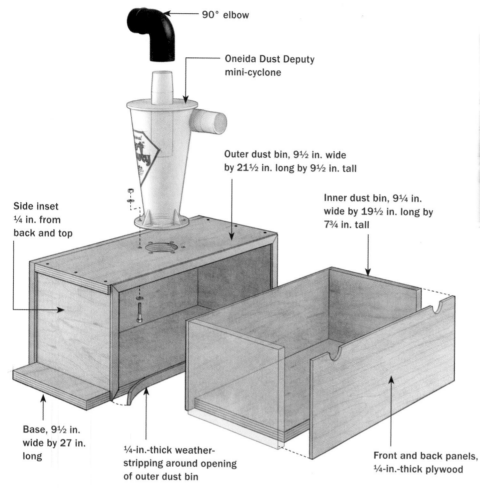

90° elbow

Oneida Dust Deputy mini-cyclone

Outer dust bin, 9½ in. wide by 21½ in. long by 9½ in. tall

Inner dust bin, 9¼ in. wide by 19½ in. long by 7¾ in. tall

Side inset ¼ in. from back and top

Base, 9½ in. wide by 27 in. long

¼-in.-thick weather-stripping around opening of outer dust bin

Front and back panels, ¼-in.-thick plywood

Fine-tune the air seal

A door on the cabinet presses tightly against weatherstripping on the dust bin, so the inner bin can be loose. Stops at the bottom and latches at the top of the door create even pressure.

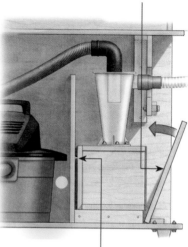

Use drywall screws on the back of the dust bin to push it back and forth to fine-tune how much the weatherstripping is compressed by the door.

The base is a dust collector

It's not too difficult to cut accurate parts from plywood. (For a few tips, see "Best-Ever Outfeed Table" on p. 125.) I'll skip over that process now and just explain how the parts go together.

I put the vacuum and the mini-cyclone in the base for two reasons: First, enclosing the vacuum muffles it. Second, it makes the bench a self-contained unit. There's no vacuum trailing behind it like a baby elephant behind its mother.

Start assembling the base with the bottom panel, predrilling holes for the casters. Then attach the front panel to the bottom. Screw the interior divider to the base and then to the front panel. Next, attach the back panel to the base and divider, but before you do,

Weatherstripping makes an airtight seal.
Miter the corners with a chisel after you apply
the stripping, and glue the corners together with
cyanoacrylate glue.

Put the Deputy on the case. To create an airtight seal, apply a
bead of acrylic caulk to the mini-cyclone's flange before putting it
on the bin.

Connect the vacuum to the mini-cyclone. A 90° elbow makes
the tight turn under the bench's top without restricting airflow like
a crimped hose would.

drill the ventilation hole (the power cord for
the iVAC switch also passes through this hole).

An apron runs across the top of the door
opening at both ends of the base. Each apron
is screwed to plywood cleats. The top cleat
attaches the top assembly. The side cleats
serve as door stops. After assembling the
aprons and cleats, screw them between the
front and back panels.

Then turn over the base and bolt the casters to it. Flip the cabinet back over and install
the doors. Attach the lower door stops to the

Layered top has room for clamps

This plywood top assembly has a clamping system built into it. The layered construction makes it easy to create tongued channels for the sliding benchdog blocks and a cavity for the pipe clamps.

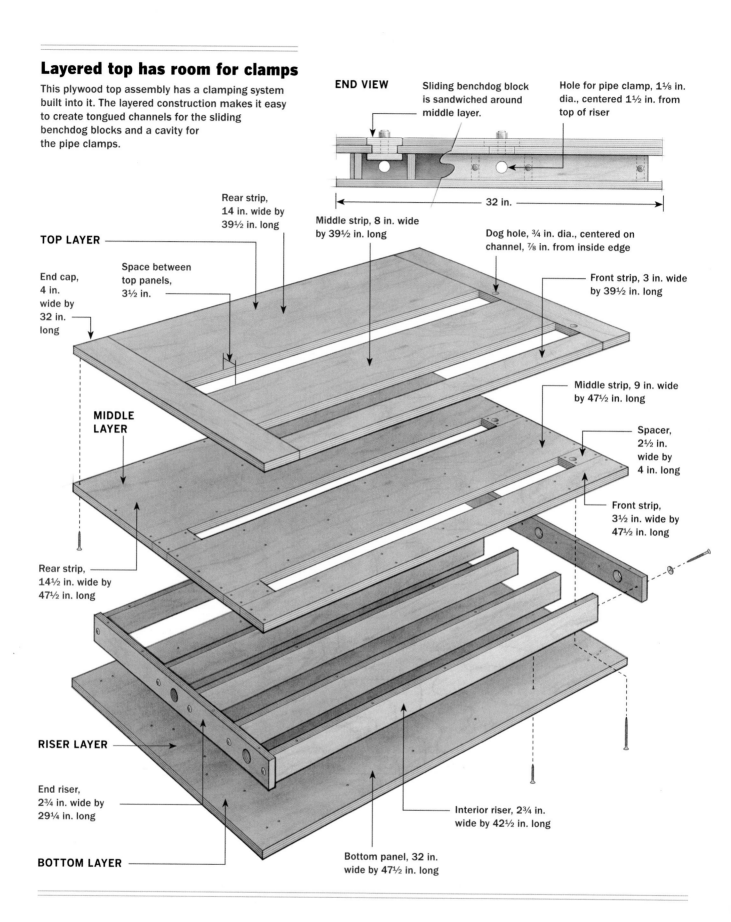

END VIEW

Sliding benchdog block is sandwiched around middle layer.

Hole for pipe clamp, 1⅛ in. dia., centered 1½ in. from top of riser

32 in.

Rear strip, 14 in. wide by 39½ in. long

Middle strip, 8 in. wide by 39½ in. long

Dog hole, ¾ in. dia., centered on channel, ⅞ in. from inside edge

TOP LAYER

Space between top panels, 3½ in.

End cap, 4 in. wide by 32 in. long

Front strip, 3 in. wide by 39½ in. long

Middle strip, 9 in. wide by 47½ in. long

MIDDLE LAYER

Spacer, 2½ in. wide by 4 in. long

Front strip, 3½ in. wide by 47½ in. long

Rear strip, 14½ in. wide by 47½ in. long

RISER LAYER

End riser, 2¾ in. wide by 29¼ in. long

Interior riser, 2¾ in. wide by 42½ in. long

BOTTOM LAYER

Bottom panel, 32 in. wide by 47½ in. long

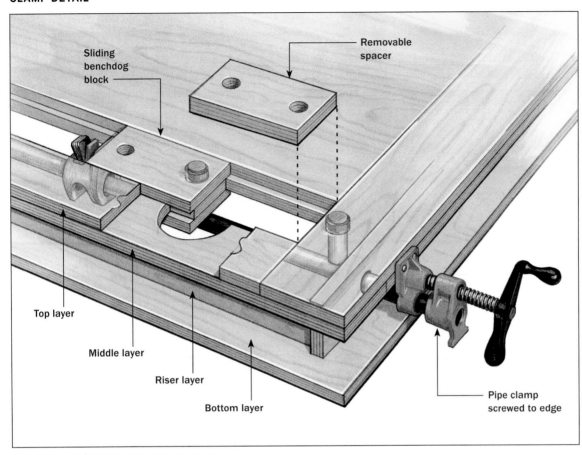

Sliding
benchdog
block

Removable
spacer

Top layer

Middle layer

Riser layer

Bottom layer

Pipe clamp
screwed to edge

sides of the cabinet and to the bottom panel. Then screw the pivoting door "locks" to the apron.

Collect the dust in an airtight box—
The Dust Deputy is a plastic cyclone typically attached to the lid of a 5-gallon bucket, which collects the chips and dust when they fall out of the cyclone. But such an assembly is too tall to fit inside the base cabinet, so I came up with another way to collect the debris. Of course, that meant overcoming a big challenge, because for the cyclone to work properly, the box needs to be airtight. Fortunately, I found an easy way to do that, because—and this is the cool part—you don't need any special tools or materials to make it.

The cyclone sits on top of a box, and inside the box is a removable drawer that catches

the dust and chips. When it is full, you just open the box, pull out the drawer, dump it in a trash can, and put it back in.

The butt joints in the box are tight enough to prevent airflow, and the door can be used to create a tight seal around the opening. Just apply foam gasket—the kind used for weather-stripping on entry doors—around the opening for the door, mitering the corners and gluing them together using cyanoacrylate glue. When the door closes against the gasket, it creates an airtight seal.

To fine-tune how much the door compresses the gasket, I drove two drywall screws into the back of the outer dust bin. Adjusting the screws in and out moves the box farther from and closer to the door and compresses the gasket less or more.

Build the top two layers first. To connect the top and middle layers, predrill and countersink for the screws and use an offcut from the plywood to keep the edges aligned as you drive the screws.

Use spacers to locate slots for clamps. Make sure they're dimensioned and placed accurately, because they determine where you drill holes for the stationary benchdogs.

Drill for the stationary benchdogs. Leave the spacers attached and drill through both pieces at once. Use scraps to support the far end of the assembly.

Add the riser frame and sliding dogs. Screw down through the frame pieces and into the top.

Finally, to complete the airtight box, apply a bead of acrylic caulk around the opening for the cyclone before bolting it in place.

The top is a vise

The cool thing about this top is that, like my new-fangled workbench, it has a clamping system built into it. All you need are two ¾-in. pipe clamps—this bench is designed for Jorgensen No. 50 Pony clamps—some ¾-in.-dia. dowel, and ¾-in.-internal-dia. vinyl tubing. The dowel is cut into short lengths to make benchdogs, and the tubing slides over the dogs to keep them from marring or denting your work, something you don't want to have happen when you're sanding a door just before applying a finish.

Here's how it works. A block of plywood with a dog hole drilled in it is pushed against the sliding jaw of the pipe clamp. The other jaw is fixed to the apron. You can move the sliding jaw wherever you need it, and the dog hole moves along with it.

The top is made from layers of plywood strips, but it is plenty rigid for power-tool work (and some hand-tool work like light planing). Screw the top and middle layers together. Mark the locations of the stationary

Make the sliding benchdog blocks

After drilling dog holes through the assembled blocks, take off the bottom layer and put the blocks in place. Three stacked pieces of blue tape, added after the dog holes are drilled, create enough play for the block to slide easily (use a knife to cut openings in the tape).

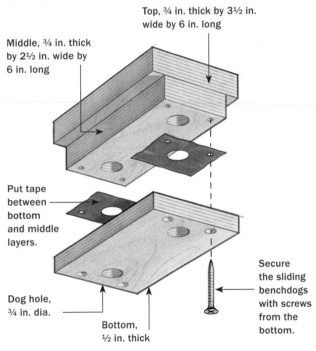

Top, ¾ in. thick by 3½ in. wide by 6 in. long

Middle, ¾ in. thick by 2½ in. wide by 6 in. long

Put tape between bottom and middle layers.

Dog hole, ¾ in. dia.

Bottom, ½ in. thick

Secure the sliding benchdogs with screws from the bottom.

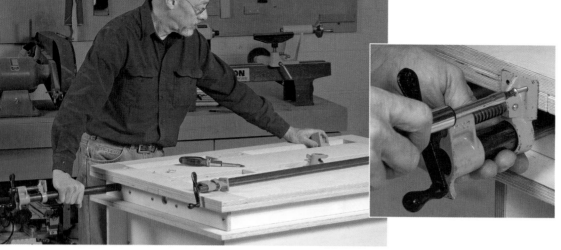

Install the pipe clamps. Put the bare end in and through the adjustable clamp head. Tighten it completely, and mark it where it's flush with the top's edge. Take it out, cut it to length, and put it back. Screw the fixed head to the bench through predrilled holes, so you can open and close it without holding the head.

Install the low-cost clamping system. Whether you're sanding or routing, the workpiece needs to be held still. White's ingenious "vise" is nothing more than ¾-in. pipe clamps and a clever system of sliding blocks and dogs, but it gets the job done and applies pressure close to the bench's surface—without sticking up and getting in the way.

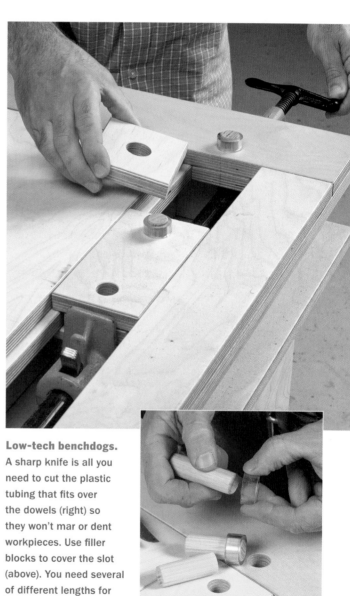

Put the top on the base. It's heavier than it looks, but one person can do it. Screw through the cleats in the base, into the top.

Low-tech benchdogs. A sharp knife is all you need to cut the plastic tubing that fits over the dowels (right) so they won't mar or dent workpieces. Use filler blocks to cover the slot (above). You need several of different lengths for complete coverage no matter where the benchdog block and clamp head are.

Tame hoses and cords from above

Nothing is more annoying than a cord or hose that continually catches and drags as you try to control a tool. White solved that problem with an overhead rack for both.

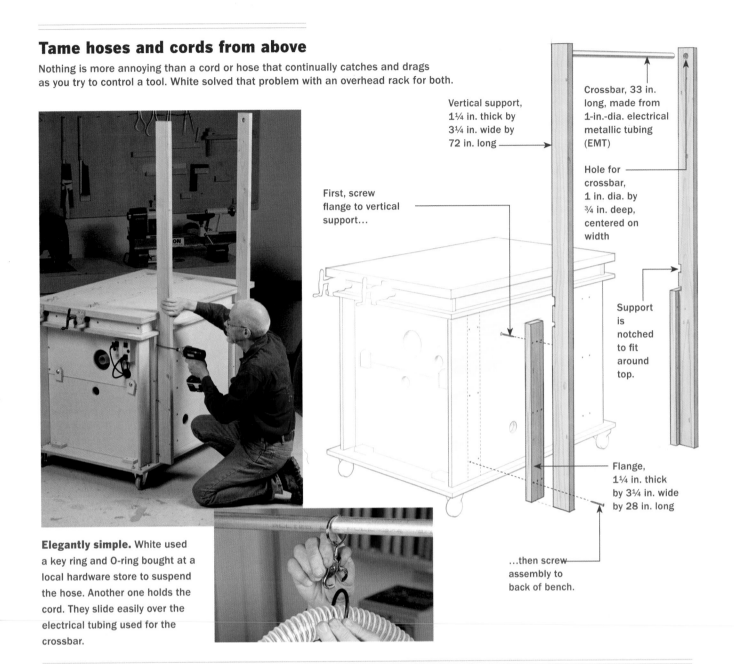

Vertical support, 1¼ in. thick by 3¼ in. wide by 72 in. long

Crossbar, 33 in. long, made from 1-in.-dia. electrical metallic tubing (EMT)

Hole for crossbar, 1 in. dia. by ¾ in. deep, centered on width

Support is notched to fit around top.

First, screw flange to vertical support...

Flange, 1¼ in. thick by 3¼ in. wide by 28 in. long

...then screw assembly to back of bench.

Elegantly simple. White used a key ring and O-ring bought at a local hardware store to suspend the hose. Another one holds the cord. They slide easily over the electrical tubing used for the crossbar.

benchdogs, partially disassemble the parts, and drill the holes.

Now that the basic structure of the top has been assembled, make and attach the riser layer. The two end risers need holes for the pipes to pass through. Drill them at the drill press.

Next, make and install the sliding bench-dog blocks. Assemble the layers and drill a hole for the benchdog. Take off the bottom layer, add some tape to make the groove a bit wider than the tongue on the top, and install the blocks. Now attach the bottom panel to the risers. Then set the entire assembly onto the base and attach it by screwing through the cleats and into the bottom panel.

Make filler blocks for the slots. Then make some benchdogs from a length of dowel and slip some vinyl tubing over one end. Finally, install the pipe clamps.

Making Sense of Vises

GARRETT HACK

A good bench vise is nearly as useful as a shop apprentice. On my bench, I have a front vise and a large tail vise—I call them my right- and left-hand men. It's hard to imagine woodworking without them; they hold my work firmly so that I can concentrate fully on powering and controlling the tool I'm using.

In general, you'll find vises at two locations on a woodworker's bench: one on the long side of the bench, typically at the left-hand corner for right-handed woodworkers, and another on the short side at the opposite end.

The first, known variously as a side vise or front vise, matches the mental picture that most people have of a vise, with a movable jaw capturing work between it and the edge of the bench.

The second, called an end vise or tail vise, can clamp work like a front vise, but is more often used to hold boards flat on the bench, pinched between a pin or dog in the vise and another in one of the many holes along the benchtop. Together, these two vises can meet all of a woodworker's basic needs when it comes to holding work firmly and within reach.

Up front: a vise to clamp work vertically or on edge

A front vise, typically found on the bench's left-front corner, is ideal when you need to clamp a board to plane an edge, hold a chair leg while shaping it, or hold a board upright for sawing dovetails. The most common design is quite simple: a jaw of wood, or cast iron lined with wood, that moves with a single screw and a T-handle. The rest of the vise is mortised into the front edge of the bench. Mine opens about 10 in. and has about 4 in. of depth.

Many of the front vises on the market are fairly easy to fit to a benchtop. Look for one that has a large screw with well-cut Acme threads. These are the same square threads found on good clamps; they can smoothly deliver lots of force over a long life.

To hold long boards, wide panels, or doors securely on edge in a front vise, you need the added support of the deep front apron of the bench. Properly installed, the fixed half of the vise should be mortised into the bench so that the movable jaw clamps against the apron. This creates a great deal of stability, making it possible to clamp most boards on edge with no other support. For very long boards, just put one end in the front vise and rest the other on a short board clamped in the tail or end vise, much like a board jack on traditional benches. You can clamp a large tabletop vertically against the front edge of a bench, one end held in the front vise and the other held by a bar clamp across the bench.

A problem can arise, though, when clamping on just one side of the vise, such as when holding just the end of a much larger piece, clamping pieces vertically for laying out

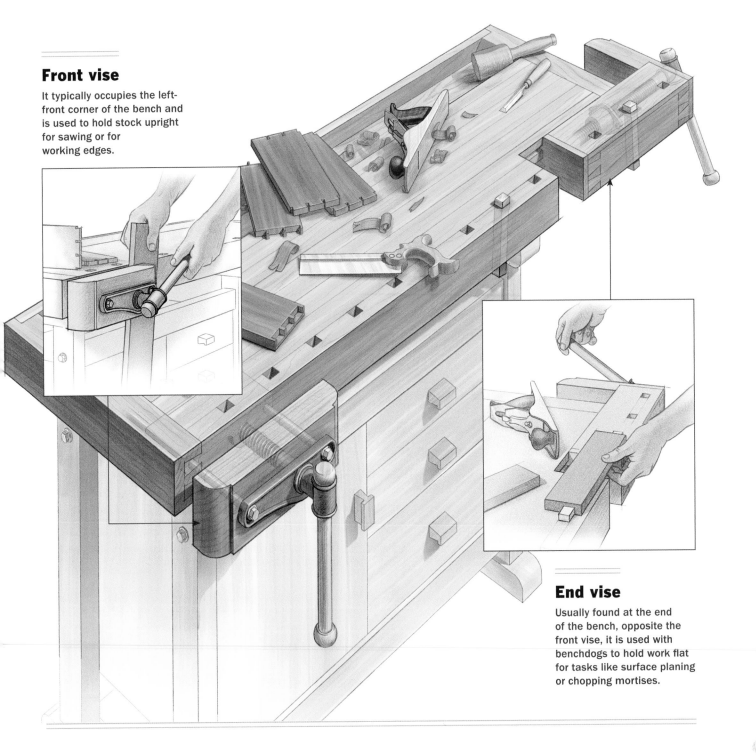

Front vise

It typically occupies the left-front corner of the bench and is used to hold stock upright for sawing or for working edges.

End vise

Usually found at the end of the bench, opposite the front vise, it is used with benchdogs to hold work flat for tasks like surface planing or chopping mortises.

or sawing dovetails, or holding tapered or oddly shaped pieces. When one side of the jaw is applying all the pressure—or trying to—it is very hard on the screw and any alignment rods, and can even distort them. One solution is to slip a block as thick as the workpiece into the other side of the jaw (use a wedge for odd shapes). This keeps the jaws parallel so you can apply all the pressure you need. Some bench manufacturers equip their front vises with a threaded stop that does the same job.

A front vice holds work vertically for sawing dovetails or planing end grain. A scrap piece of similar thickness, clamped in the opposite side of the vise, prevents the vise from racking.

Hold wide workpieces on edge. The vise screw prevents a wide piece from going all the way through the vise (top). A clamp seated in a dog hole provides extra support (above).

Secure long boards on edge. A block clamped in the tail vise supports the opposite end.

Steady a wide panel. A sawhorse provides support underneath, with the opposite end clamped to the bench apron.

Types of front vise

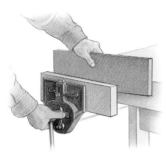

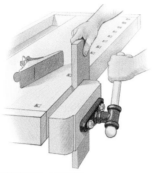

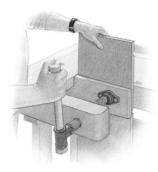

CAST IRON

The most popular front vise is cast iron. A steel rod or two keep the jaw aligned. Some also have a quick-action release for faster jaw adjustments.

WOODEN-JAWED

A wooden-jawed vise operates like its cast-iron cousin. The movable jaw is typically made from the same material as the bench. Some models offer a quick-release option.

ARM VISE

An arm vise works well on wide boards. There are no screws or rods in the way. But the right-angled arm limits clamping force, which reduces the ability to clamp long boards horizontally.

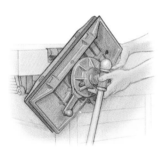

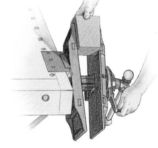

PATTERNMAKER'S VISE

A patternmaker's vise can hold oddly shaped work at any angle. The vise body can pivot up and over the bench until the jaws are parallel to the benchtop. The jaws also can rotate 360° and angle toward one another for holding tapered work.

Build it yourself. Many companies sell the hardware for these vises. Look for a large screw with square-cut threads.

At the end: a vise to hold work flat

At the other end of the bench, you typically will find one of two distinct types of vises, known as end vises or tail vises. Their main purpose is to hold work flat on the surface of the bench.

A traditional tail vise, with one row of dog holes along the front edge of the bench and several more in the movable jaw, allows you to hold work flat over nearly the entire length of the bench. This is ideal for holding long boards to smooth a face, bead one edge, or hold a leg while chopping a mortise. You can also clamp across the grain to bevel a panel end or shape the skirt of a chest side. Be careful to apply only modest pressure to hold the work, or you will bow it up.

An end vise holds work flat. Aligned with a row of dog holes, this vise has a wide capacity. It can hold smaller work and pieces nearly as large as the benchtop. It's ideal for smoothing a tabletop.

A secure grip for cross-grain work. The end vise allows you to clamp a panel across its width for tasks such as planing a bevel on the end.

For chopping, a spacer keeps the work off the vise jaw. The pounding could damage the vise. The best support is on the benchtop itself, right over a leg.

An end vise also handles awkward shapes. Pieces like this curved table apron can be held securely for scraping or other tasks.

The tail vise is also great for holding long or odd pieces at any angle—there are no screws in the way and the hefty construction tends to prevent racking on odd shapes. Also, it can hold a workpiece at right angles to the bench edge, ideal for planing an end-grain edge, shooting a miter on a molding, or paring a tenon shoulder.

One drawback with this vise is that the large movable jaw can sag. A misaligned jaw makes it difficult to hold work flat on the benchtop. Avoid chopping or pounding over the movable jaw; it isn't as solid as the benchtop itself. Support the work as much as possible over the bench, with the least amount of jaw open. I keep small, square blocks handy to shim my work toward the bench or protect it from the dogs. I shouldn't have to say this, but never sit on your tail vise.

Types of end vise

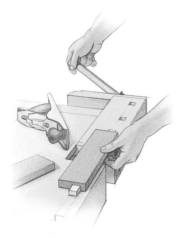

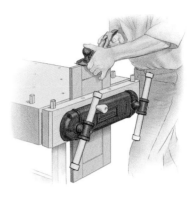

CAST IRON

Same vise, different location. The cast-iron front vise also works well as an end vise—a smart solution if you have room or money for only one vise.

TAIL VISE

The traditional end vise. The movable jaw is a thick section of the bench's front edge, about 18 in. long. Dog holes hold work flat on the surface. The jaws also can hold work at an angle.

TWIN-SCREW

A twin-screw model can clamp wide stock vertically. A chain connects the two screws to prevent racking.

FULL WIDTH

A modern variation spans the width of the bench. With two rows of dog holes, the wide jaw of this vise is ideal for holding wider panels.

The guts.
Tail-vise hardware comes with instructions for making the wood components.

Another type of end vise—The other popular type of end vise looks and works like a front vise, except that the movable jaw is mounted to, and set parallel with, the end of the bench. If I had to outfit a bench with just one vise, it would be this type (see drawing, top left). My small traveling bench has an old front vise mounted on one end in line with a row of dog holes.

Some end vises of this type have a jaw that spans the entire width of the bench. Equipped with a dog on each end of the jaw, and paired with a double row of dog holes down the front and back of the bench, this is a great system for holding wide parts flat on the benchtop. Several ready-made benches are built this way. Lee Valley also sells the necessary hardware for making the vise yourself.

Your Miter Saw Needs a Stand

JOHN WHITE

These days, a miter saw in the workshop is about as common as a router. Woodworkers use the saw for everything from cutting up rough lumber to making perfect-fitting compound-miter cuts for a cabinet crown molding. I designed this stand to take care of just about any demand your miter saw throws at you.

A good stand can make any miter saw sing a sweeter song. This one has five features that make it stand out from the rest, turning a portable carpentry tool into a safer and more accurate woodworking machine. One feature we don't point out at right is how easy this cabinet is to build, with just two sheets of ¾-in.-thick plywood and a box of drywall screws.

Support for long pieces. Each fence extends outward by 15 in. That's helpful when you want to set up the stop for extra-long workpieces. A short shelf on each end supports those long boards (and cutoffs).

Small footprint. To make the stand compact, White designed folding side tables. When not in use, just pivot the support gussets out of the way to lower the hinged tables.

Full mobility. White added four casters to make the stand easy to roll around, a useful feature when the shop must give way to the family car. Available at Grizzly Industrial (www.grizzly.com), the casters swivel and include a brake.

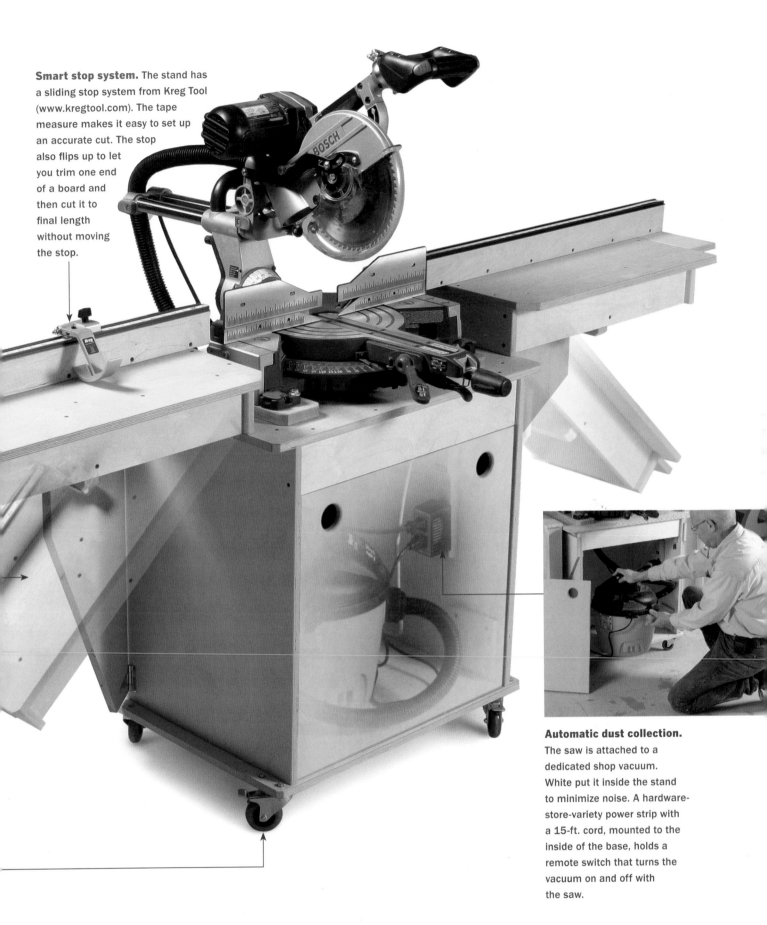

Smart stop system. The stand has a sliding stop system from Kreg Tool (www.kregtool.com). The tape measure makes it easy to set up an accurate cut. The stop also flips up to let you trim one end of a board and then cut it to final length without moving the stop.

Automatic dust collection. The saw is attached to a dedicated shop vacuum. White put it inside the stand to minimize noise. A hardware-store-variety power strip with a 15-ft. cord, mounted to the inside of the base, holds a remote switch that turns the vacuum on and off with the saw.

The base is the foundation

Quick work. White uses a trim router with a ¼-in.-radius roundover bit to soften the edges on all the parts, including the holes drilled in the front and back of the base.

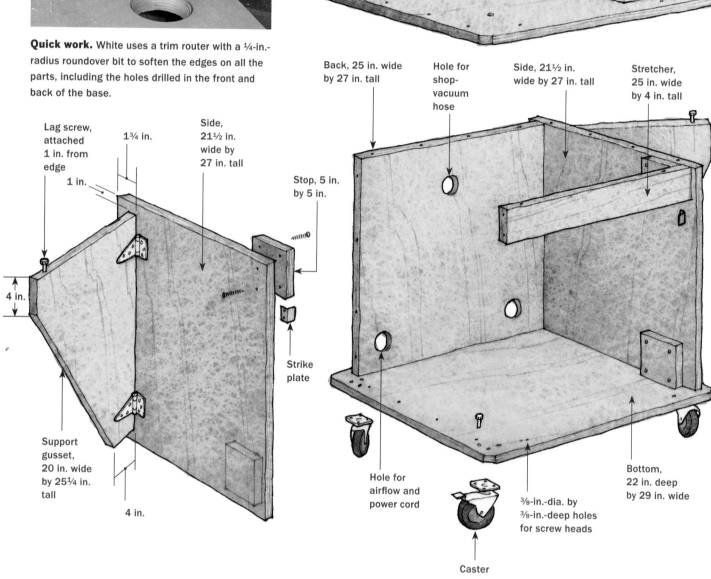

Filler block, 4 in. wide by 15½ in. long, thickness to suit

Top, 22 in. deep by 30½ in. wide

Lag screw, attached 1 in. from edge

1¾ in.

1 in.

Side, 21½ in. wide by 27 in. tall

Back, 25 in. wide by 27 in. tall

Hole for shop-vacuum hose

Side, 21½ in. wide by 27 in. tall

Stretcher, 25 in. wide by 4 in. tall

Stop, 5 in. by 5 in.

4 in.

Strike plate

Support gusset, 20 in. wide by 25¼ in. tall

4 in.

Hole for airflow and power cord

Caster

⅜-in.-dia. by ⅜-in.-deep holes for screw heads

Bottom, 22 in. deep by 29 in. wide

GET ALL THE PARTS FROM TWO SHEETS OF ³/₄-IN. PLYWOOD

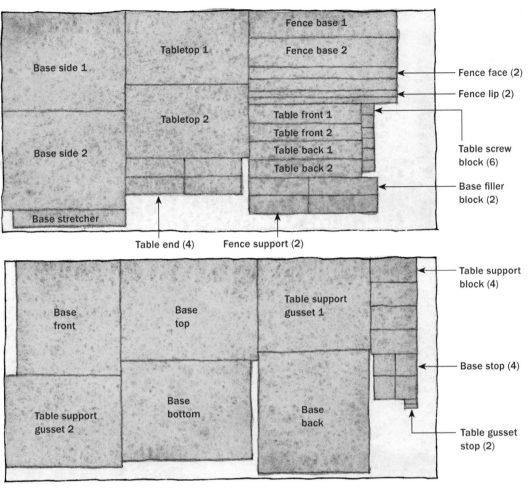

Base side 1

Tabletop 1

Fence base 1

Fence base 2

Fence face (2)

Fence lip (2)

Base side 2

Tabletop 2

Table front 1

Table front 2

Table back 1

Table back 2

Table screw block (6)

Base filler block (2)

Base stretcher

Table end (4)

Fence support (2)

Base front

Base top

Table support gusset 1

Table support block (4)

Table support gusset 2

Base bottom

Base back

Base stop (4)

Table gusset stop (2)

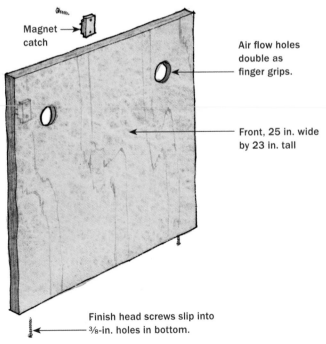

Magnet catch

Air flow holes double as finger grips.

Front, 25 in. wide by 23 in. tall

Finish head screws slip into ³/₈-in. holes in bottom.

Start by making the base

The base supports the saw and holds the vacuum. It also serves as a platform for the tables and fences that are attached later.

I made the stand so the saw table would be at a height of 32½ in. That works for most people. But you can adjust the height to suit your needs.

Determine the base dimensions for your saw—The stand shown is designed to accept a Bosch 10-in. sliding compound-miter saw. Depending on the size of your saw, the length and width of your base might be bigger or smaller.

Clearance hole first. Each screw requires a shank hole and a shallow countersink for the screw head.

Pilot hole next. Align the parts and drill pilot holes into the plywood edges below. This makes them much less likely to split.

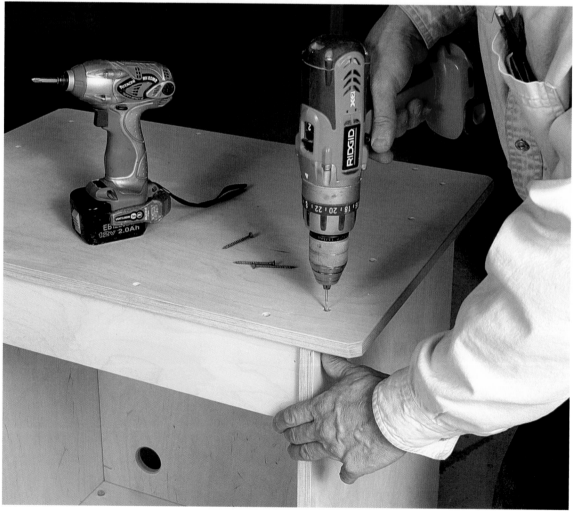

No glue needed. Drywall screws provide plenty of holding power, so there's no need to fuss with glue.

For other saws, there's an easy way to determine the side-to-side (length) and front-to-back (depth) dimensions of the top of the base. With the saw on your workbench, swing the blade all the way to the left and mark the extreme left-hand location of the saw handle. Then swing the saw all the way to the right and mark the extreme right-hand location of the handle. Measure the distance between the marks and add 2 in. This is the length of the top of the base.

To determine the depth of the base top, allow 9½ in. from the front edge of the top to the front face of the miter-saw fence. Then, at the back edge, add enough depth to ensure that all four of the miter saw's feet will end up on the surface.

Now you're ready to build. All of the base parts are joined with drywall screws. Drill an 11/64-in.-dia. shank hole and a 3/32-in.-dia. pilot hole for each screw.

The back and front have a series of 2-in.-dia. holes for the vacuum hose and for airflow and power cords. The holes in the front panel also work as finger grips. I used a drill press and a Forstner bit to drill the holes, although a hole saw also can do the job.

Once the stand is assembled, mount the four casters. To avoid having a bolt run into the bottom edge of the front and back panels, I used only three bolts to mount each caster, not the normal four.

Add the side tables and fences

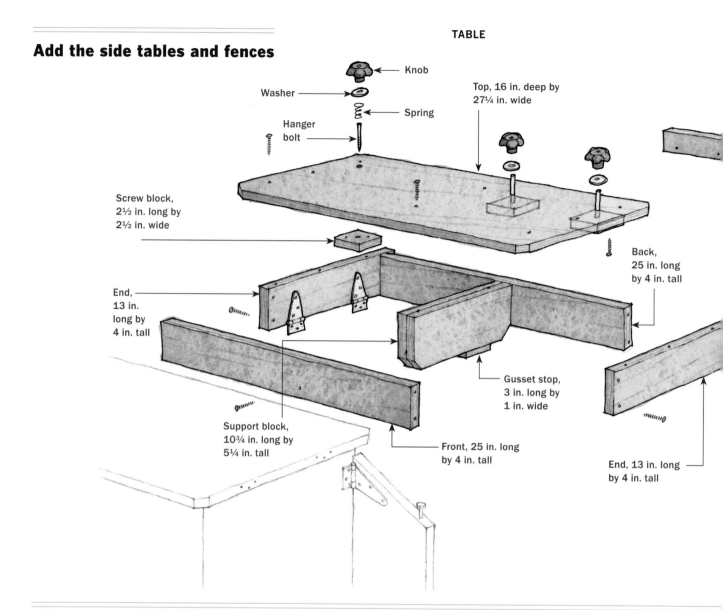

Knob

Washer

Spring

Hanger bolt

Top, 16 in. deep by 27¼ in. wide

Screw block, 2½ in. long by 2½ in. wide

End, 13 in. long by 4 in. tall

Back, 25 in. long by 4 in. tall

Gusset stop, 3 in. long by 1 in. wide

Support block, 10¾ in. long by 5¼ in. tall

Front, 25 in. long by 4 in. tall

End, 13 in. long by 4 in. tall

Make the two side tables

As with the base, the side tables are assembled with drywall screws. The support block in the center of each table is actually two pieces of stock face-glued together to make a single 1½-in.-thick piece. Cut the block to fit snugly between the front and back pieces of the tables. Add the stop, which positions the support gusset when it's under the table. Then mount a support block to each table by driving screws through the table sides and into the ends of the blocks.

For additional reinforcement, drive a couple of screws down through the top.

Now mount the hinges, made by National Manufacturing Co. (www.natman.com, part No. N128-512). I bought them at a local hardware store and used the same kind to mount the tables and the support gussets. Next, cut the support gussets to size. A lag screw in each gusset allows you to adjust the tables parallel with each other. Check that the lag screw hits the stop at about the front-to-back midpoint of the table.

FENCE

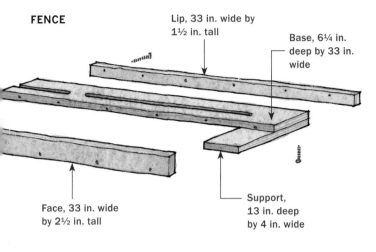

Lip, 33 in. wide by 1½ in. tall

Base, 6¼ in. deep by 33 in. wide

Face, 33 in. wide by 2½ in. tall

Support, 13 in. deep by 4 in. wide

Assembly tip. A stop block clamped to the ends of the table makes it easier to establish the ½-in. inset for the front and back pieces.

TOP VIEW

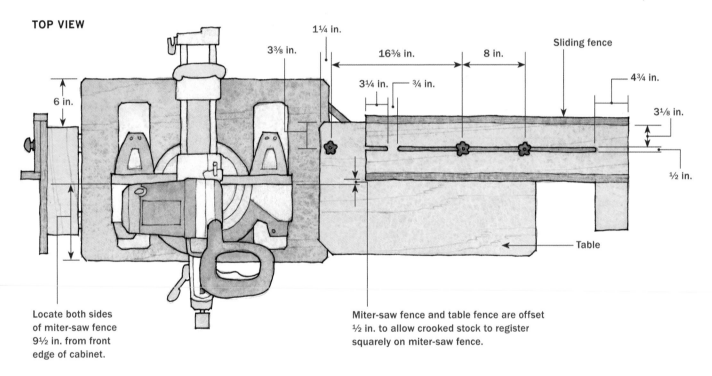

1¼ in.

3⅜ in.

16⅜ in.

8 in.

Sliding fence

6 in.

3¼ in.

¾ in.

4¾ in.

3⅛ in.

½ in.

Table

Locate both sides of miter-saw fence 9½ in. from front edge of cabinet.

Miter-saw fence and table fence are offset ½ in. to allow crooked stock to register squarely on miter-saw fence.

To level the saw table with the side tables, install filler blocks on top of the base. Use solid stock so you can plane down the blocks until the miter-saw table is flush with the stand tables. Using filler blocks here gives you some room for height adjustment if you happen to replace your saw.

When bolting the saw in place, locate the holes so the miter-saw fence ends up 9½ in. from, and parallel to, the front edge of the cabinet. Cut the bolt holes oversize so you can make adjustments to the saw location before locking it down.

Cut the grooves. With a ½-in.-dia. straight bit in the router table and an outside fence acting like a featherboard, White makes the short end-groove cut first (left). To create the long stopped groove, the stock is slowly lowered into the bit from above, then fed forward or backward as needed to complete the groove.

Assemble the lip and face. After the base of the fence is grooved, the lip and face are screwed in place.

The fences hold the stop blocks

The base of each fence has two grooves— one long, one short—to accept the hanger bolts and knobs. These allow the fences to slide outward to support long boards. After assembling the fence parts, place a fence on each table and mark the location of the hanger bolts. Drill ¹¹⁄₆₄-in.-dia. holes for the ¼-in. bolts. To better support the bolts, screw blocks under each one. When driving in the hanger bolts, use two nuts on each of them so you can drive them with a wrench. Add the washers and nuts and check the fences for a smooth sliding fit.

The Kreg® track is next. Measure the fence, then use a hacksaw to cut the track to that length. Drill a few holes through the back of the track and use the supplied screws to mount it to the fence. Do the same on the other fence. Mount the measuring tape and the lift-up stop. Now you have the best chopsaw stand on the block.

Best-Ever Outfeed Table

JOHN WHITE

A good outfeed table is essential for safe woodworking because it allows you to control the workpiece as it moves past the blade and off the back of the tablesaw.

Without it, you'll have to push down hard on the back of long boards, which makes it difficult to guide them safely past the blade. An outfeed table also naturally doubles as a work surface for assembly and finishing. But the space beneath the table often lies unused, a wasted opportunity for efficient storage.

This outfeed table has a cabinet below that takes advantage of that space, with dedicated storage areas for the rip fence, miter gauge, crosscut sled, blades, and several big drawers for jigs. And there's plenty of shelf space for general storage, as well as room on the end panels for clamps. The large phenolic-plywood top is great because it's so slick that materials almost float across it. And because the surface resists stains and glue, it's perfect for assembly and finishing. I let the top overhang the base for easier clamping.

It's easy to adjust the table's height and level it, too. So if you move to a new shop, you won't need a new table.

Best of all, this outfeed table is not difficult to build. The hardest part may be dealing with the large sheets of plywood, but I'll offer tips that make breaking down and squaring the material easier. All of the joinery is simple. The cabinet itself is joined by butt joints held together by screws (I'll offer pointers on assembling the joints accurately). The drawers are joined by a rabbet-and-groove joint that requires only two tablesaw setups.

Materials improve function and ease construction

This cabinet is built entirely of sheet goods, except for two Douglas-fir runners. The top, drawer fronts, and kick plates come from a single 4x8 sheet of phenolic plywood. The cabinet is ¾-in.-thick Baltic-birch plywood, and the drawers are ½-in.-thick Baltic-birch plywood.

The entire table can be made more economically from medium-density fiberboard (MDF) or ordinary plywood, but you'll have to use connecting bolts with barrel nuts to make strong joints in the softer MDF. With plywood, you can use screws. And you'll need to apply a finish to the tabletop to toughen it and seal it against stains and glue.

Shelve your sled.
A dedicated shelf keeps
the crosscut sled out of
the way but easily
accessible.

No wasted space. You
can do glue-ups and other
bench tasks on this table,
so you'll need tools and
supplies nearby.

Blades at the ready.
The bottom drawers are
deep enough to store blades
vertically, making them
easier to identify and
pull out.

Stow your fence.
A well-placed rack keeps the
rip fence close at hand.

Basic anatomy

Baltic-birch and phenolic plywood combine for good looks, a sturdy base, and a low-friction top. Adjust the height shown here to fit your saw.

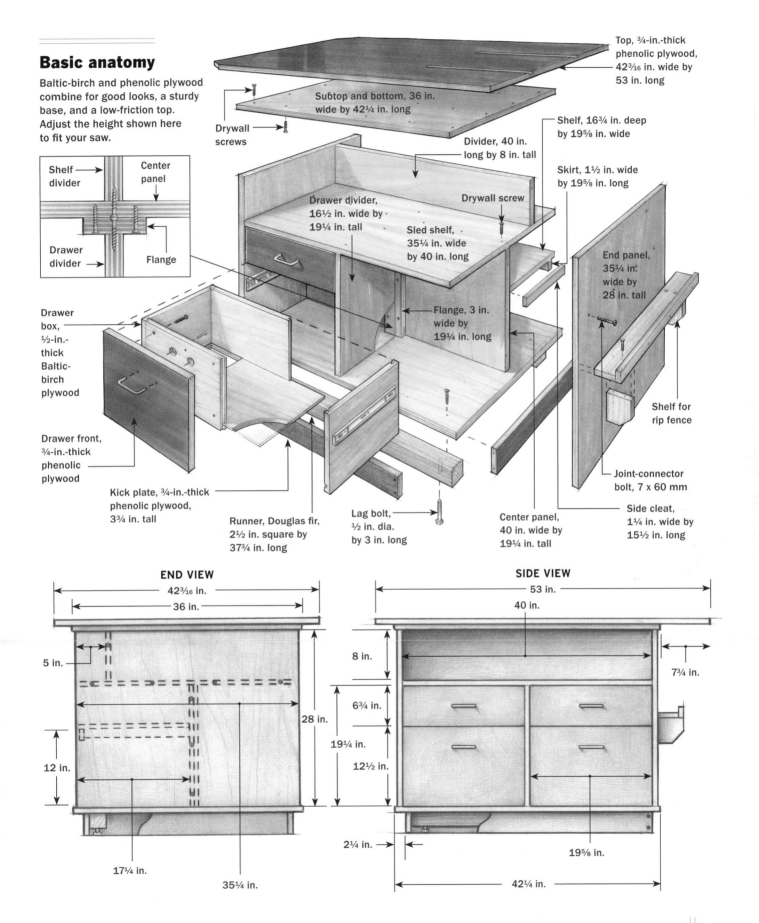

Top, ¾-in.-thick phenolic plywood, 42³⁄₁₆ in. wide by 53 in. long

Subtop and bottom, 36 in. wide by 42¼ in. long

Drywall screws

Divider, 40 in. long by 8 in. tall

Shelf, 16¾ in. deep by 19⅝ in. wide

Drawer divider, 16½ in. wide by 19¼ in. tall

Drywall screw

Skirt, 1½ in. wide by 19⅝ in. long

Sled shelf, 35¼ in. wide by 40 in. long

End panel, 35¼ in. wide by 28 in. tall

Shelf divider

Center panel

Drawer divider

Flange

Drawer box, ½-in.-thick Baltic-birch plywood

Flange, 3 in. wide by 19¼ in. long

Shelf for rip fence

Drawer front, ¾-in.-thick phenolic plywood

Joint-connector bolt, 7 x 60 mm

Kick plate, ¾-in.-thick phenolic plywood, 3¾ in. tall

Runner, Douglas fir, 2½ in. square by 37¾ in. long

Lag bolt, ½ in. dia. by 3 in. long

Center panel, 40 in. wide by 19¼ in. tall

Side cleat, 1¼ in. wide by 15½ in. long

END VIEW

42³⁄₁₆ in.

36 in.

5 in.

28 in.

12 in.

17¼ in.

35¼ in.

SIDE VIEW

53 in.

40 in.

8 in.

7¾ in.

6¾ in.

19¼ in.

12½ in.

2¼ in.

19⅝ in.

42¼ in.

Precise plywood pieces

Use a circular saw and guide to square up factory-cut edges and to cut parts to a manageable size for the tablesaw.

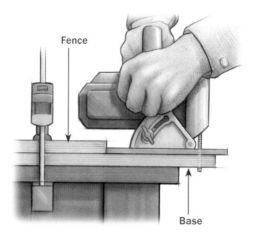

Fence

Base

Make a cutting guide. Attach a fence to a slightly oversize base. Then trim the guide with a circular saw to establish a dead-accurate reference for lining up cuts.

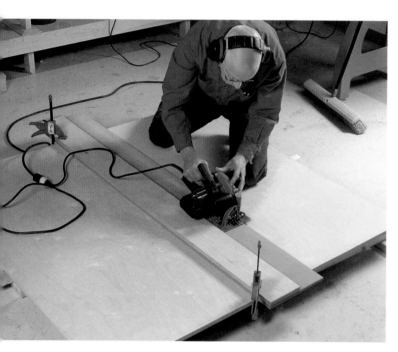

How to use it. Align the guide so that the first cut not only gives you a straight side, but also a square corner.

Clamping tip. When trimming the panel square, use a bar clamp to help hold it against the fence. A block at either end helps keep the clamp in position.

Joinery tips

Careful layout of joint locations and a few well-placed brads take the fuss and frustration out of butt joints. The layout lines show you where to drill, and the brads act as a third hand to hold the panels steady as you mark screw locations.

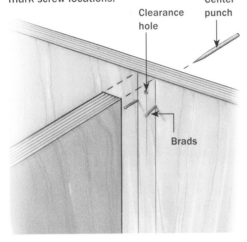

Clearance hole

Center punch

Brads

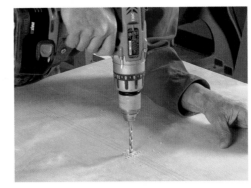

Drill along the centerline. Two lines show the edges of the intersecting panel. The third line marks the centerline for the clearance holes.

Brads are helping hands. Brads driven in along the edge lines will hold the intersecting panel in place as you transfer the location of the clearance holes. A pair at the top and at the bottom is all you need.

Transfer the pilot-hole locations. With the two panels aligned and held in place, slide a center punch through the outer panel and tap it to mark locations for the pilot holes. Disassemble the parts and drill the holes.

A guide for square panels

You can't rely on the factory-cut edges being square to each other, and full sheets are hard to handle on the tablesaw anyway. Solve both problems by using a circular saw and cutting guide to break down the sheet into smaller workpieces.

Set the guide so that it cuts an edge square to a factory edge. Use a sanding block to clean up the two square edges and then measure and mark the panel's final dimensions. Trim it to size on the tablesaw, running the square edges along the fence.

Bevel all edges on the panels with a chamfer bit. This prevents damage to the panels and adds a bit of safety. A square phenolic edge is very sharp and easily can cut you. Beveled edges also create crisp shadow lines at the joints, which I like.

Use a drill to start the screws. Drive in the joint-connector bolts, leaving them about ⅛ in. proud of the panel.

Hand torque brings them home. Use an Allen wrench to drive the bolts flush with the panel. A drill might over-drive the head or strip the pilot hole.

Screw joints are solid

All of the table's joints, except those in the drawers, are simple butt joints held together with screws. Where they wouldn't be visible, I used drywall screws. Where the screw heads are exposed, I used joint-connector-bolt wood screws (www. mcfeelys.com, #1423-CWB), which have large, bronze-colored heads that

look good on shop furniture. Although these are called bolts, they're actually hefty wood screws that need aligned clearance and pilot holes drilled before you drive them home (see photos on p. 129 and above).

Butt joints can be hard to align and assemble, so I use a couple of tricks to make things easier. First, I mark where one panel butts

A logical order for assembly. Start with the core, assembling the end and center panels and tracing their locations onto the bottom. Next, mark centerlines, drill holes for the drywall screws, and then attach the bottom.

Add the dividers. Attach the shelf divider first. Then install the flange (see drawing, p. 127) and drawer divider.

The sled shelf is next. Drive joint-connector bolts through the end panels into the sled shelf. Use drywall screws to secure the shelf to the drawer and shelf dividers.

Flip the cabinet to attach the feet. Lag bolts screwed into Douglas-fir runners make easily adjustable feet. After flipping over the cabinet, attach the runners with drywall screws.

against the other. With these lines drawn, it's easy to tell where the joint is located and to drill accurate clearance or pilot holes along the centerline.

Once the clearance holes are drilled, you need to transfer their centers onto the edge of the intersecting panel so that you can drill pilot holes. But it's not easy to hold everything in alignment when you do that, so I drive a few brads into the edge lines drawn earlier to trap the panel and hold it steady while I transfer the centers. I pull out the brads with a claw hammer when the joint is together. The layout lines and small nail holes left behind are hidden inside the case.

Assemble the table in stages

I built my table in stages to avoid accumulated errors, but some parts should be cut in groups for uniformity. The cabinet's center panel can be cut at the same time as

Make way for the miter gauge. Put the outfeed table in place—leveled and adjusted to the right height—and use the saw's miter gauge to locate the clearance slots.

Screws shouldn't show. After the table has been righted and the subtop attached, you can put the phenolic top in place. Secure it from below with drywall screws. That way, its smooth surface is unbroken except for the miter slots, which provide clearance for gauges and sleds.

Rout the clearance slots

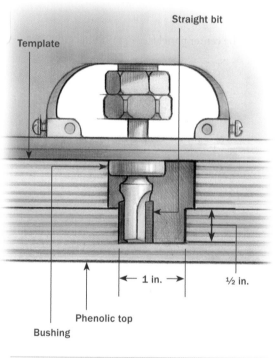

Template

Straight bit

Phenolic top

Bushing

1 in.

½ in.

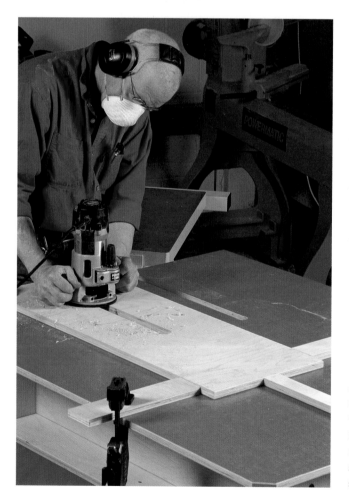

Jig makes quick work of wide slots. White used a router equipped with a guide bushing and straight bit to cut the clearance slots. His method produces a wide, accurate slot without having to move a straightedge for multiple passes.

the drawer and shelf dividers because they need to be the same height.

Begin by assembling the end panels and the center panel (see top left photo on p. 131). Once they're joined and square to one another, get the dimensions for the bottom and subtop by measuring the assembly and adding ¾ in. to its width and length. The bottom and subtop overhang the core assembly by ⅜ in. on all four sides, which makes it easier to fit them because the alignment of the edges won't need to be exact. Attach the bottom, but not the subtop.

The drawer and shelf dividers are next. The shelf divider is simply screwed to the center panel. The back of the drawer divider, however, has a strip of plywood attached to it. Screws are then driven through the resulting flange to attach the drawer divider to the center panel (see detail on p. 127). This is necessary because once the shelf divider is installed, you won't be able to drill through the center panel to attach the drawer divider.

After the dividers are in place, install the large shelf that provides storage for the sled. When you screw it down, keep the drawer and shelf dividers square to the center panel. Next, add the divider that serves as a back to the shelf.

You're now ready to attach the subtop, which adds stiffness to the phenolic top and makes it easier to screw it on. Before you attach it, drill and countersink a series of holes for the screws that will attach the phenolic top to the base. Drill them 6 in. apart around the subtop's perimeter and about 2 in. from the edge. Do the same around the center. Now, attach the small shelf on the side of the table. To keep things simple, I screwed the shelf to a pair of cleats, which are hidden by a skirt on the front edge.

Flip over the base and attach the two runners that receive the table's lag-bolt feet.

These runners are made from Douglas-fir 4x4s trimmed to 2½ in. square. Drill pilot holes for the lag-bolt feet and screw them in, leaving them about 1 in. proud of the runners. The lag bolts allow you to adjust the table's height and to level it. Attach them 2¼ in. from the edge of the bottom.

Flip the base back over and attach the phenolic top (see top left photo on facing page). In addition to beveling the edges of the panel, I trimmed the two corners opposite the saw at 45°, which is easier to do with the top attached.

Next, level the cabinet and bring the top in line with the saw's table. Then transfer the location of the miter slots directly from the saw table and mark them out on the top. Mine are ½ in. deep by 1 in. wide by 20⅝ in. long. To cut the channels, you only need a router, a straight bit, and a straightedge, but I made

Simple joinery, sturdy drawers

Build the whole drawer box with just two tablesaw setups, one for the grooves and one for the rabbets.

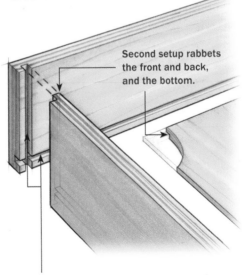

Second setup rabbets the front and back, and the bottom.

First setup cuts dadoes for the front and back, and grooves for the bottom panel.

1. Dadoes and grooves

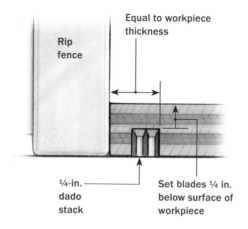

Rip fence

Equal to workpiece thickness

¼-in. dado stack

Set blades ¼ in. below surface of workpiece

Dadoes in the sides. Use a miter gauge to guide the drawer sides safely along the rip fence.

Grooves for the bottoms. Run the bottom of the sides, fronts, and backs against the fence to cut the groove for the bottom panel.

2. Rabbets

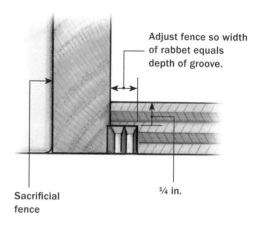

Adjust fence so width of rabbet equals depth of groove.

Sacrificial fence

¼ in.

Rabbet the fronts and backs. With the dado head buried in a sacrificial fence, cut the rabbets for the corner joints.

Rabbet the bottom panels. All four sides of the bottom panels are rabbeted to fit into the grooves running around the bottom of the drawer box.

Assembly is easy. Go easy on the glue to avoid squeeze-out. Use brads to hold things snug as the glue dries.

Check for a consistent gap. The outfeed table should be a hair below the saw table. Hold a straightedge firmly down on the tablesaw to check.

a template and used an offset guide bushing, which allowed me to rout the entire channel without having to adjust a straightedge to get the full width (see drawing on p. 132).

For dust clearance, I drilled a ¾-in.-dia. hole about 6 in. from the end of each channel. The dust falls into the gap between the back of the saw and the outfeed table.

A fast drawer joint that lasts

You can build the drawer boxes in a variety of ways, but I recommend a rabbet-and-groove joint that requires only two setups on the tablesaw (see drawing on p. 133). These

drawers are quite strong and can be made in short order.

The drawer boxes are made from Baltic-birch plywood that's just a hair under ½ in. thick, but that doesn't mean the joint is harder to cut. You'll cut all of the dadoes and grooves with the first setup and all of the rabbets with the second (see photos on facing page). The dadoes, grooves, and rabbets are cut with a ¼-in. dado stack set at the same height, so you'll only need to reset the fence between setups.

The easiest way to assemble the drawers is to brush a small amount of glue on the rabbets (you want to avoid squeeze-out) and tack the joints together with two or three small brads. The brads will hold the joint snug as the glue dries. Clamping is time-consuming,

Quick adjustments. The coarse thread of the lag-bolt test makes for speedy height adjustments.

Add a kick plate. Phenolic kick plates and drawer fronts are durable, but also give the cabinet a unified look and subtle pop. The plate hides the feet and stops things from rolling under the cabinet. It's easy to remove to make height adjustments.

Install the false fronts. Use shims and double-faced tape to position each drawer front, and then screw it on from the inside.

and the weight and pressure of the clamps can throw the drawer out of square.

I used standard ball-bearing, full-extension slides from a home center to mount the drawers in the outfeed table.

Attach the drawer fronts and kick plate

Fit the fronts with the table in place and adjusted for height and level. The table might twist a bit as a result of the adjustments, and you'll get a better fit after them.

The four pieces of the kick plate are screwed to one another at the corners but aren't attached to the cabinet. This makes them easy to remove should you need to tweak the table's height if you move the saw and table.

A few coats of shellac on the Baltic-birch plywood will give it some protection.

Your newly minted outfeed table will make your shop safer and better organized. And that will make your woodworking more enjoyable.

Pivoting Plywood Cart

MICHAEL PURYEAR

I build a variety of furniture using solid wood, veneer, and plywood, and since I work in a one-man shop, I constantly look for ways to make the experience as easy and efficient as possible. One of these ways is my panel cart. With this cart, I can stop struggling with 4x8 sheet goods such as medium-density fiberboard (MDF) and plywood, and easily move them about the shop. And because I built the cart to the height of my tablesaw, I can tilt the sheets horizontally to feed them directly from the cart onto the tablesaw.

Large swivel casters, a brake, and a steering handle make for easy maneuvering. A simple design and very basic joinery, tied together with bolts, make this a project that easily can be built in a day, so you can get right back to making furniture. Next to its usefulness, the best thing about this cart is that the materials are relatively inexpensive. Because you can use dimensioned construction lumber and/or scraps you have kicking around the shop, the cost is limited and mostly for the hardware.

Using the cart

I load 4x8 sheets on the panel carrier side and rough lumber on the other. I can then move the cart around the shop wherever it is needed, and it doesn't disturb the lumber when I tilt the sheet goods to the horizontal position. The four swivel casters allow me to push the cart in any direction without having to turn it around, and the handle lets me tow the loaded cart.

The cart lets me store, move, and rip up to eight 4x8 sheets. With multiple sheets stacked on the cart, the top sheet will be higher than your tablesaw when you tilt the sheets up into position. But you can still slide it onto the saw table and cut it safely. When you lift the pivoting frame, two latches lock it into position.

Move and cut large panels with ease

Roll. Large wheels and a pull handle help you tow a heavy load. Note that the back side can hold a pile of rough lumber. A foot brake locks the cart in place.

Pivot. Tip the support frame that holds the sheet goods into the horizontal position, where it locks automatically. Then move the cart into position and apply the brake.

Push. The cart supports the back end of the plywood, freeing you up to feed the material and apply pressure against the fence.

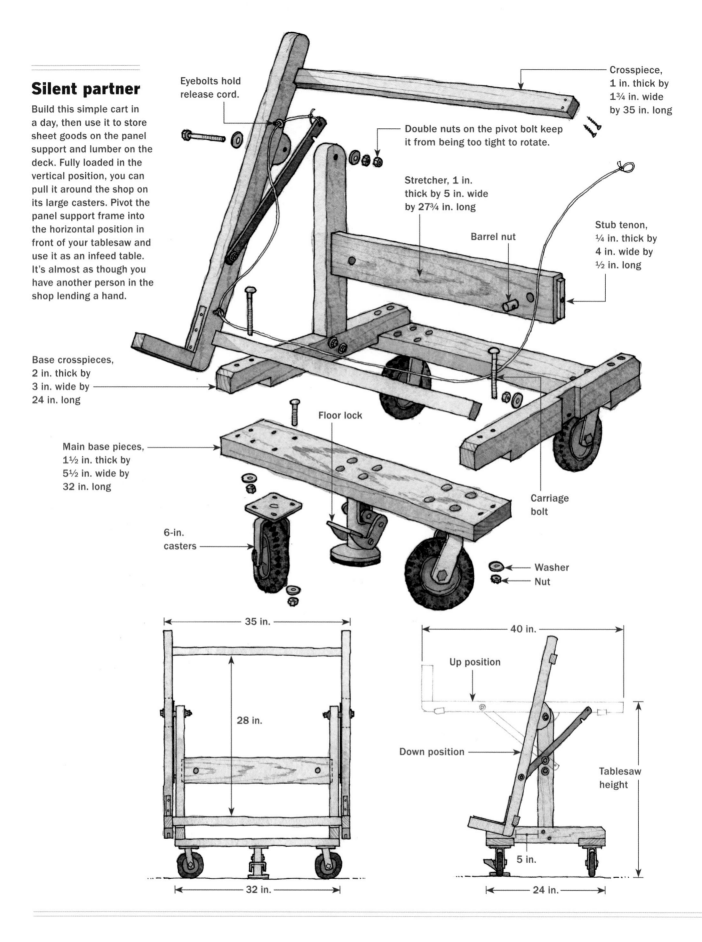

Silent partner

Build this simple cart in a day, then use it to store sheet goods on the panel support and lumber on the deck. Fully loaded in the vertical position, you can pull it around the shop on its large casters. Pivot the panel support frame into the horizontal position in front of your tablesaw and use it as an infeed table. It's almost as though you have another person in the shop lending a hand.

Eyebolts hold release cord.

Crosspiece, 1 in. thick by 1¾ in. wide by 35 in. long

Double nuts on the pivot bolt keep it from being too tight to rotate.

Stretcher, 1 in. thick by 5 in. wide by 27¾ in. long

Barrel nut

Stub tenon, ¼ in. thick by 4 in. wide by ½ in. long

Base crosspieces, 2 in. thick by 3 in. wide by 24 in. long

Floor lock

Main base pieces, 1½ in. thick by 5½ in. wide by 32 in. long

6-in. casters

Carriage bolt

Washer

Nut

35 in.

28 in.

32 in.

40 in.

Up position

Down position

Tablesaw height

5 in.

24 in.

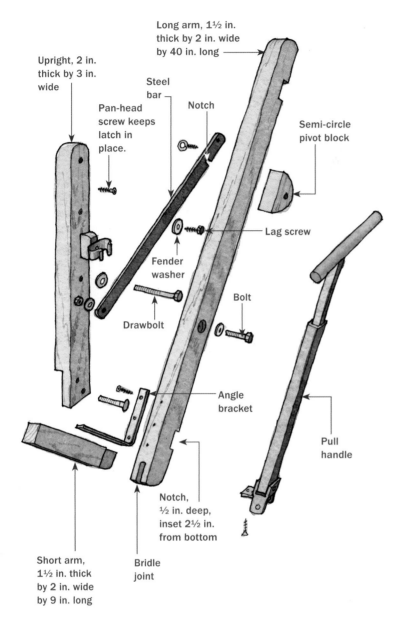

Upright, 2 in. thick by 3 in. wide

Pan-head screw keeps latch in place.

Steel bar

Notch

Long arm, 1½ in. thick by 2 in. wide by 40 in. long

Semi-circle pivot block

Lag screw

Fender washer

Drawbolt

Bolt

Angle bracket

Pull handle

Notch, ½ in. deep, inset 2½ in. from bottom

Short arm, 1½ in. thick by 2 in. wide by 9 in. long

Bridle joint

Set the pivot height

The frame's height is important. It can be a little higher than the tablesaw height, but not lower.

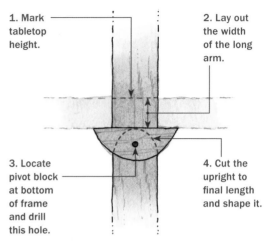

1. Mark tabletop height.

2. Lay out the width of the long arm.

3. Locate pivot block at bottom of frame and drill this hole.

4. Cut the upright to final length and shape it.

Take time to get it right. Once the base frame is built, add the casters and clamp an upright to the base. Adjust a marking tool to the tablesaw table. Puryear uses an Accuscribe from FastCap®, and then he transfers that mark to the upright.

Assemble the base. Connect the four base pieces, attach the casters, and add the stretcher and two uprights.

To lower the pivoting frame, you pull a cord to release the latches and lower the structure. What a pleasure not having to wrestle sheet goods onto the tablesaw when working alone.

A very basic base with casters

The base construction is simple. Except for the mortises in the uprights, I cut all of the joinery on the tablesaw. To line up everything perfectly, cut both crosspieces at once, clamping them together and using a miter

Locate the panel support. After making the two L-shaped pieces and notching them for the crosspieces, but before gluing in the crosspieces, you need to locate the Ls on the uprights. To do this, bolt a semicircle pivot block to its upright, and clamp one of the Ls to the base (top) so its lower crosspiece will hit the base about 5 in. from the upright. Mark the block's location on the L.

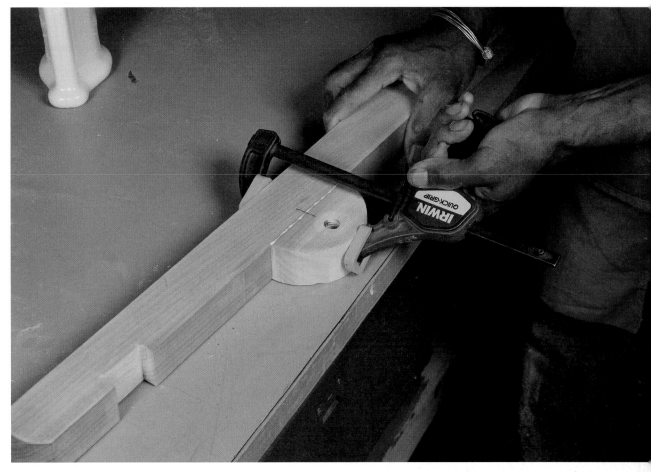

Glue on the pivot block. With the pivot blocks marked for position, glue and clamp one to each L. Now you can glue in the crosspieces to complete the panel support frame.

gauge and dado blades with multiple passes. The uprights that hold the tilting panel support frame determine the final height of the cart in its horizontal position. Base their length on your caster height and the height of your tablesaw. Right now, cut them longer than you will need until you settle on a final height (a little later in the process).

The bottom end of each upright gets a half-lap that corresponds with the half-lap in the base of the crosspieces. Each upright also gets a centered mortise (cut with an edge guide on a router) to hold the stub tenon of the stretcher. I reinforce this joint with a draw-bolt. I clamp the stretcher to the uprights and drill through both for the drawbolt and barrel nut. Once this joinery is cut, bolt the

casters and the crosspieces to the main base. Don't attach the uprights yet.

This is a good time to talk about the casters. The loaded cart can get heavy. I use four heavy-duty 6-in. swivel casters rated at 330 lb. each, which are not available with total locking brakes. In lieu of brakes, I added a floor lock. I prefer all four casters to swivel because it makes maneuvering around the shop easier. I wouldn't use casters smaller than 5 in., because small obstacles on the floor will stop them dead.

Tilting panel support affects the height of the uprights

To build the panel support frame, start by making the two L-shaped pieces. Cut the

Connect the panel support frame to the base. Nuts and bolts with washers on either side keep things together (above left). The notch in the latch rests on a lag screw between a washer and the upright (above right). An extra screw will act as a stop and keep the latch from jumping out of line. The washer guides the bar back in place.

notches for the crosspieces using a dado blade. The elbow is a bridle joint that I reinforced with angle brackets because they will carry all the weight of the 4x8 sheets.

To determine the height, clamp an upright to the base. Roll this assembly up to your tablesaw and mark the height of the table on the upright.

Then move to the bandsaw and cut two semicircular pivot blocks from 1½-in.-thick lumber and drill a hole centered between the corners and 1 in. from the flat side. Clamp each block to its upright with the flat side parallel to and 2 in. below the line marked as the tablesaw height. Center the hole in the block on the upright and drill through it into the upright. Repeat for the second upright.

Now the pivot blocks are located on the uprights so that they will hold the support frame level with the top of the tablesaw when the frame is tilted to the horizontal position.

Cut the uprights to length, radius their tops, and bolt each one to the base. Then round over the top and bottom of each L (for aesthetic purposes only). Once that's done, insert a bolt through one pivot block and into its upright. Rest one of the Ls on the block and adjust it so that the bottom of the lower crosspiece will land on the base 5 in. from the upright. Clamp the L to the base and then to the pivot block and mark the block's location on the L. Transfer the marks to the other L and glue the blocks in place.

Simple release. A cord that runs from the end of one latch around the frame through eyebolts and to the end of the second latch is pulled to lift the latches, releasing the panel frame so it can pivot into the vertical position.

Latch system holds panel support horizontally

For the latch system, I use two steel bars (available at most hardware stores). I drill holes on each end and use a hacksaw to turn one hole into a notch (I also drill a smaller hole for the release cord). One end gets screwed to the L of the support, and the notched end hooks over a lag screw in the upright. To mark the latch's bolt hole on the L, pivot the panel support horizontal and level and place the latch notch over the lag screw on the upright. Drill the bolt holes, then bolt the latches loosely in place so they move easily using locking nuts. Place pan-head screws on the uprights above each latch so that the latches can disengage but not rise above the fender washer. Leave ⅛ in. between the head and the upright.

Because I can't unhook both of those bars and hold the cart support while it's pivoting, I attached a cord that runs between the bars and allows me to unhook them at the same time. Finally, attach a pull handle to one end of the cart.

Sources

DRAWBOLTS AND BARREL NUTS
www.leevalley.com
(No. 05G07.01)

PULL HANDLE
www.harborfreight.com
(No. 94354)

FLOOR LOCK AND CASTERS
www.globalindustrial.com
(No. CJ241851, lock;
No. WB601122, casters);

www.harborfreight.com
(No. 41565, casters)

House Your Tools in High Style

CHRIS GOCHNOUR

Atool cabinet is a great shop helper. It keeps hand tools and small power tools well organized and off the bench but within reach. And perhaps more importantly it saves valuable floor space. But a tool cabinet doesn't have to have the cold feel and look of MDF or the piecemeal appearance of a cabinet made entirely from scraps. Rather, it can have the look of fine furniture, giving tools an attractive home and your shop an aesthetic boost.

I collaborated with the editors at *Fine Woodworking* to design a useful, attractive tool cabinet. It can be built with the most basic shop tools in a short amount of time, and it will beautify your shop as it has mine.

The carcase, made of ¾-in. walnut plywood, is built with simple dado joinery cut with a tablesaw. The six interior drawers employ a similar setup. The attractive doors couldn't be easier to make. They feature stub-tenon and groove joints for the frame, a veneered plywood panel glued in place, and divided glass panes that can be done in no time at all. Construction starts with the case.

A blend of sheet goods and solid wood

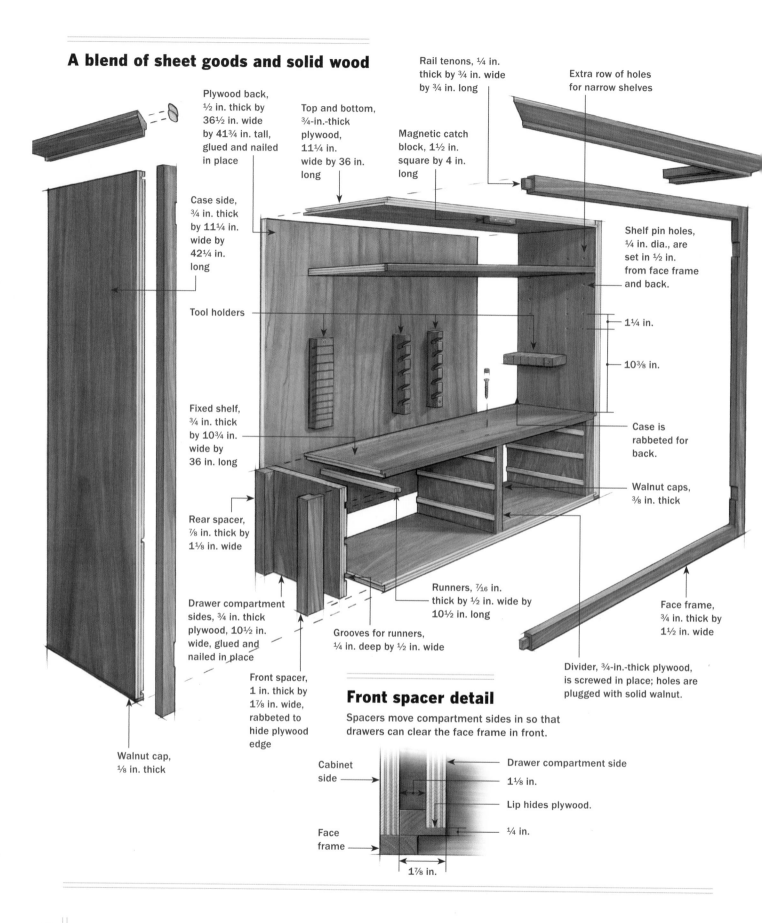

Rail tenons, ¼ in. thick by ¾ in. wide by ¾ in. long

Extra row of holes for narrow shelves

Plywood back, ½ in. thick by 36½ in. wide by 41¾ in. tall, glued and nailed in place

Top and bottom, ¾-in.-thick plywood, 11¼ in. wide by 36 in. long

Magnetic catch block, 1½ in. square by 4 in. long

Case side, ¾ in. thick by 11¼ in. wide by 42¼ in. long

Shelf pin holes, ¼ in. dia., are set in ½ in. from face frame and back.

Tool holders

1¼ in.

10⅜ in.

Fixed shelf, ¾ in. thick by 10¾ in. wide by 36 in. long

Case is rabbeted for back.

Walnut caps, ⅜ in. thick

Rear spacer, ⅞ in. thick by 1⅛ in. wide

Drawer compartment sides, ¾ in. thick plywood, 10½ in. wide, glued and nailed in place

Runners, ⁷⁄₁₆ in. thick by ½ in. wide by 10½ in. long

Face frame, ¾ in. thick by 1½ in. wide

Grooves for runners, ¼ in. deep by ½ in. wide

Divider, ¾-in.-thick plywood, is screwed in place; holes are plugged with solid walnut.

Front spacer, 1 in. thick by 1⅞ in. wide, rabbeted to hide plywood edge

Walnut cap, ⅛ in. thick

Front spacer detail

Spacers move compartment sides in so that drawers can clear the face frame in front.

Cabinet side

Drawer compartment side

1⅛ in.

Lip hides plywood.

Face frame

¼ in.

1⅞ in.

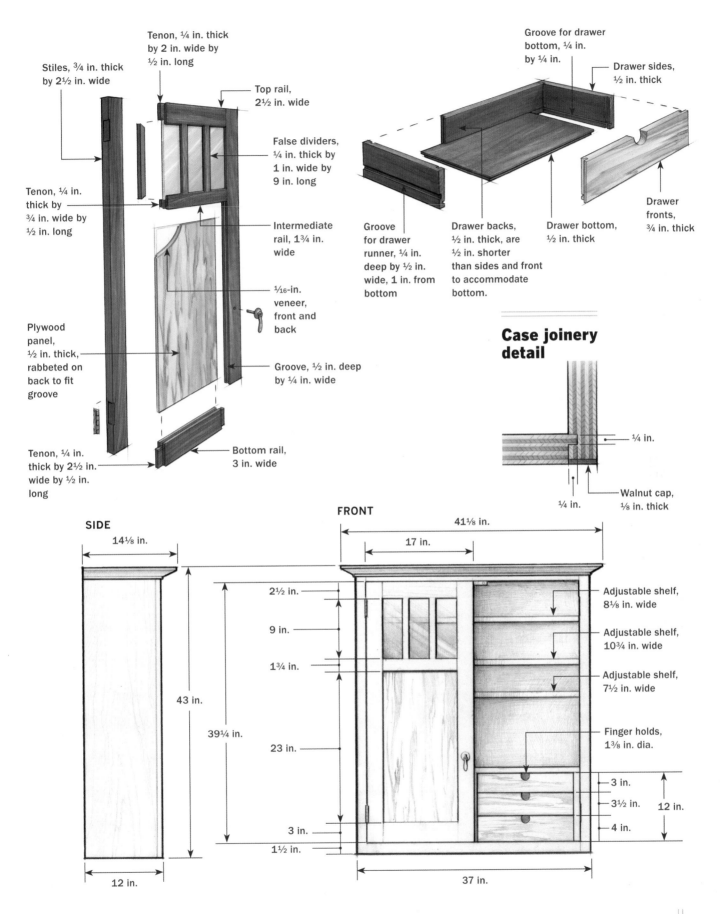

Tenon, ¼ in. thick
by 2 in. wide by
½ in. long

Stiles, ¾ in. thick
by 2½ in. wide

Top rail,
2½ in. wide

False dividers,
¼ in. thick by
1 in. wide by
9 in. long

Tenon, ¼ in.
thick by
¾ in. wide by
½ in. long

Intermediate
rail, 1¾ in.
wide

1⁄16-in.
veneer,
front and
back

Plywood
panel,
½ in. thick,
rabbeted on
back to fit
groove

Groove, ½ in. deep
by ¼ in. wide

Tenon, ¼ in.
thick by 2½ in.
wide by ½ in.
long

Bottom rail,
3 in. wide

Groove for drawer
bottom, ¼ in.
by ¼ in.

Drawer sides,
½ in. thick

Groove
for drawer
runner, ¼ in.
deep by ½ in.
wide, 1 in. from
bottom

Drawer backs,
½ in. thick, are
½ in. shorter
than sides and front
to accommodate
bottom.

Drawer bottom,
½ in. thick

Drawer
fronts,
¾ in. thick

Case joinery detail

¼ in.

¼ in.

Walnut cap,
⅛ in. thick

SIDE

14⅛ in.

43 in.

39¼ in.

12 in.

FRONT

41⅛ in.

17 in.

2½ in.

9 in.

1¾ in.

23 in.

3 in.

1½ in.

Adjustable shelf,
8⅛ in. wide

Adjustable shelf,
10¾ in. wide

Adjustable shelf,
7½ in. wide

Finger holds,
1⅜ in. dia.

3 in.

3½ in.

12 in.

4 in.

37 in.

No help needed. The case is fairly large, but with carefully fitted joints, the glue-up shouldn't require more than two hands.

Case is a lesson in tablesaw joinery

All of the main components of the case (including the adjustable shelves) can be built from one sheet of ¾-in.-thick walnut plywood. The back is ½-in.-thick walnut plywood. Some suppliers may be reluctant to sell a partial sheet of hardwood plywood. If your supplier won't, and you don't think you'll use the cutoff in the future (or make two cabinets!), you can make a solid-wood back.

Begin with the case sides. Cut them to length but leave them ¼ in. extra-wide. Glue ⅛-in.-thick solid walnut caps to the bottom edges and trim them flush. After that, rip the sides to their final width. The fixed shelf also is edged with solid walnut that's trimmed flush prior to cutting the joinery.

The case dado joints are cut on the table-saw with a ¼-in.-wide dado blade. Adjust the blade for a ¼-in.-deep cut and make the dadoes in the sides for the top, the bottom, and the fixed shelf. Then, without changing the height or width, cut the ¼-in. tongues on the top, the bottom, and the fixed shelf. Now cut the rabbets that will house the cabinet back. I do this on a router table using a straight bit and a fence to guide the cut. The rabbets on

Face frame is last. After gluing and nailing in the back, attach the face frame to the front (left). Trim it flush with a router (below) after the glue dries.

Build the drawer compartment. Install the spacers and compartment sides after cutting the dadoes for the drawer runners. The center divider is screwed in from above and below. Temporary plywood spacers on each side (top and bottom) keep the divider aligned vertically.

the case sides are stopped, while those on the top and bottom run all the way through.

With all the joints cut, you can dry-fit and then glue up the assembly. Gluing in the plywood back as you assemble the carcase will help keep things square. Reinforce the assembly with brad nails.

Crown molding in four cuts

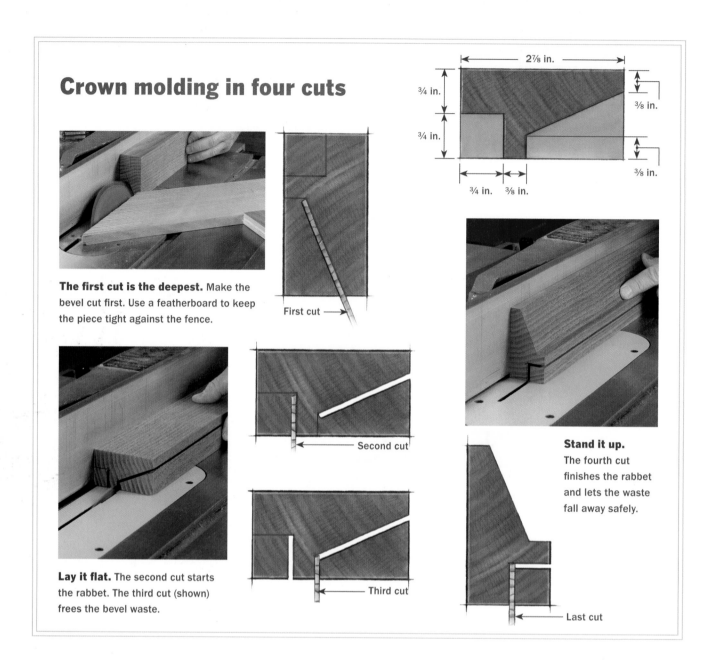

The first cut is the deepest. Make the bevel cut first. Use a featherboard to keep the piece tight against the fence.

First cut →

2⅞ in.

¾ in.

¾ in.

⅜ in.

⅜ in.

¾ in.   ⅜ in.

← Second cut

Lay it flat. The second cut starts the rabbet. The third cut (shown) frees the bevel waste.

← Third cut

Stand it up. The fourth cut finishes the rabbet and lets the waste fall away safely.

← Last cut

Face frame and crown are solid walnut

I make the face-frame parts a hair oversize in width so they overhang the case by about ¹⁄₃₂ in. all the way around. This makes it a bit easier to get the frame aligned and squared perfectly. The stiles and rails are joined using mortises and tenons. I remove the bulk of the mortise waste at the drill press and finish with chisels. The tenons are cut on the tablesaw using a dado blade.

Glue up the frame and then glue it to the case (see left photo on p. 151). Once the frame is aligned the way I want, I drive four brads, one in each corner, to ensure that the frame doesn't shift as I clamp it. After the glue has set, flush-trim the frame to the case.

The crown molding is very easy to make and apply. It is made using four different tablesaw setups (see "Crown Molding in Four Cuts" above). Make the profile and clean up the cuts with scrapers and sandpaper, then

Don't change the blade.
Reset the height of the dado blade to cut the stub tenons. Dial in the tenon with a test piece, then crank out the tenons on all the parts.

Center the grooves. The door frames are grooved for the glass and the wooden panel. To make sure the groove is centered, cut it in two passes with a dado blade, flipping each workpiece end for end after the first pass.

Spacers help the glue-up. Because the glass is installed later, the intermediate rail is hard to align and keep square. Gochnour uses spacers to align the piece before clamping it (above). The panel is glued all around, adding strength to the door (right). To avoid squeeze-out, brush glue into the grooves but not on the panel.

cut the miters and fit the molding. I reinforce the miters with #10 biscuits, and then glue and nail the molding to the case. The adjustable shelves are plywood with solid walnut edging. I made two of the shelves shallower to make it easier to access tools without banging a shelf edge.

Scraper trick gets the reveal just right. Before tightening down the clamps, use a card scraper as a lever to adjust the reveal all around the rabbet on the back of the door panel.

Glass sits in a rabbet. With the door face-down, remove the wood behind the groove, using a bearing-guided rabbeting bit riding on the wood in front of the groove. Square up the corners.

Spacers again. The false dividers are cut for a tight fit and butt-joined to the frame. When gluing them in, use spacers to align them correctly.

Wood plugs add strength

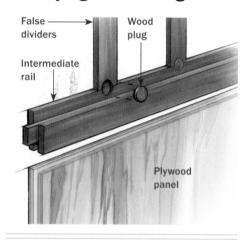

False dividers

Wood plug

Intermediate rail

Plywood panel

Holes for the plugs. Gochnour uses wood plugs to reinforce the small butt joints. Drill ⅛-in.-deep mortises for them using a ½-in.-dia. Forstner bit.

Dirt-simple glass doors

The frame-and-panel doors have three divided lights in the upper section, but their construction isn't complicated: It's all tongue-and-groove joinery, with the plywood panel glued in place for strength.

After milling the frame material, cut the panel grooves on all the inside door parts (see top left photo on p. 153). The grooves also receive the rail stub tenons, which are cut using a dado blade on the tablesaw.

The ½-in.-thick plywood panel on my cabinet doors is covered with spalted syca-more veneer. But you can substitute a nice hardwood plywood. Cut the panel to size and rabbet the back on the tablesaw to form a tongue that is captured by the groove of the door frame. Once all the parts are cut and fitted, glue up the doors.

The glass in the top of each door is an eye-catching detail, and my method of installing the single pane of glass is easy. First, rout a rabbet for the glass using a bearing-guided rabbeting bit (see top left photo above) and square the corners using a chisel. The false dividers are butt-joined to the frame rails.

Cut and release. Use a plug-cutter to make a row of ½-in.-dia. plugs in a walnut blank and then rip off a thin strip on the bandsaw to free them.

Glue them in. Align the plug's grain with that on the dividers, and trim the plugs flush after the glue dries. The frame is attached with brads.

Add the glass after finishing. It is held in place with a small bead of adhesive caulk below the glass and a thin mitered frame (left) attached with brads. Drill pilot holes for the brads, and use a sheet of thin cardboard to protect the glass as you drive them home (above).

More tablesaw joinery. After cutting the grooves for the side runners, cut the narrow dadoes for all of the drawer backs. Keep the blade at the same height but adjust the fence to cut the dadoes for all of the drawer fronts.

Simple drawer joinery

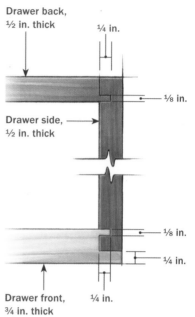

Drawer back, ½ in. thick

¼ in.

⅛ in.

Drawer side, ½ in. thick

⅛ in.

¼ in.

Drawer front, ¾ in. thick

¼ in.

Hold it steady. The tongues on the drawer backs are cut flat on the saw table with a dado blade. To cut the tongue and rabbet joint in front, hold the workpiece upright as shown, using a featherboard and tall fence to keep the piece from tipping.

Bite the tongue. After dialing in the setting, trim the tongues on all the drawer fronts.

Cut them to width, and then carefully fit them lengthwise. The butt joint is reinforced from behind with a ½-in.-dia. long-grain plug.

The opaque glass I use is called "domestic seedy," purchased from a local glass dealer. It is held in place with adhesive caulk and a thin mitered frame.

Drawers are quick to make

The six drawers in the cabinet are side hung and require a couple of extra vertical panels on both sides of the drawer compartment. Those pieces, ¾-in.-thick plywood, are blocked out from the case sides so the drawers clear the face frame.

Cut the side panels and the center divider to size at the same time, and then cut the dadoes for the drawer runners. Now add the solid-wood edging to the center divider and trim it flush.

Now you're ready to assemble the drawer compartment. Cut and fit the spacers and glue and nail the pieces to the sides. Next, glue and nail the compartment sides to the spacers. Finally, screw the center divider in place from above and below. The screw holes are countersunk and plugged.

Once the internal case is assembled, make the maple drawer runners and fit them in their dadoes. The runners have some front-to-back play and, when dry-fitted, can slide back and forth. They butt against the back of the drawer fronts and, when glued in place, also serve as the drawer stops.

The drawers use simple dado joinery at the back and front. I made the drawer bottoms from ½-in.-thick solid alder, but you could substitute plywood there. The bottom is screwed into the drawer back, with a slot in the bottom to allow for movement.

The drawer pulls need to be flush because of the close proximity of the drawer fronts to the doors. I use a simple 1⅜-in.-dia. hole drilled into the edge of the drawer front using a Forstner bit.

Once the drawers are complete, make the tool holders and finish the piece (I used a sprayed lacquer). To hang the cabinet, simply screw right through the back, being sure you hit the wall studs. Now if only I could find the time to put away all my tools . . . .

No fitting required. The runners have enough play front to back to allow you to adjust the drawers perfectly flush in front. Glue in the runners (top) one pair at a time. Then, before the glue dries, install the drawer and tap it so that the front is perfectly flush (above). Leave it that way until the glue dries.

Keep Planes Close at Hand

CHRIS GOCHNOUR

Let's face it. Handplanes are expensive, costing as much as or more than a benchtop power tool. To keep these investments safe, many woodworkers tuck their planes inside drawers or cabinets. Though the tools are safe and sound, it's a nuisance to keep opening a door or drawer to access the planes when they're needed. For convenience, many folks end up keeping their most-used planes on top of the bench.

That method is not so convenient, however, because the planes can get in the way, and they're just inches from getting knocked to the floor accidentally. My plane rack solves all of those problems.

Though simple in design, the rack has a unique way of holding the planes. The knobs are suspended from loops made from bootlaces, and the soles rest on an angled panel. The system is strong and stable, and the bootlace hangers allow me to grab and store planes with ease.

This rack holds what I consider to be a full set of handplanes—a jointer, fore, jack, two smoothers (Nos. 4 and 4½), and three block planes—with room below for some specialty planes, such as a shoulder plane. But the rack can be modified to fit more or fewer planes or planes of different sizes.

Easy access. Planes go in and out in seconds with this easy-to-make rack.

Bootlaces are the secret

Planes rest on the angled back panel and are held in place with sturdy bootlace loops. The rack hangs on a hidden French cleat, screwed into studs.

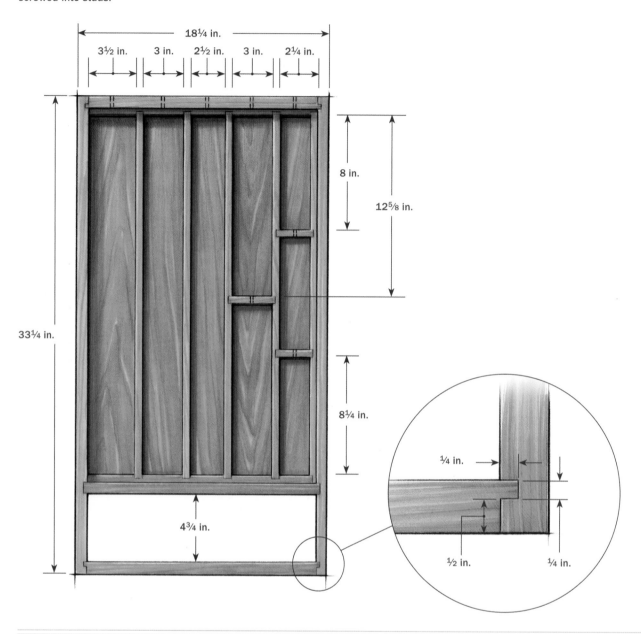

Joinery is straightforward

The case is assembled with simple dadoes and rabbeted dadoes. After cutting these joints, you can take on the trickiest part of the assembly: cutting the grooves for the angled back panel. Start by making the grooves in the underside of the top and in the top of the horizontal divider. These through-grooves

are cut on the tablesaw using a dado set tilted to the panel angle (5°). Then, dry-assemble the case. Place a spacer, the same thickness as the back panel and about 1 in. wide by 3 in. long, into the grooves in the top and divider. Knife around the spacer to locate the grooves in the sides.

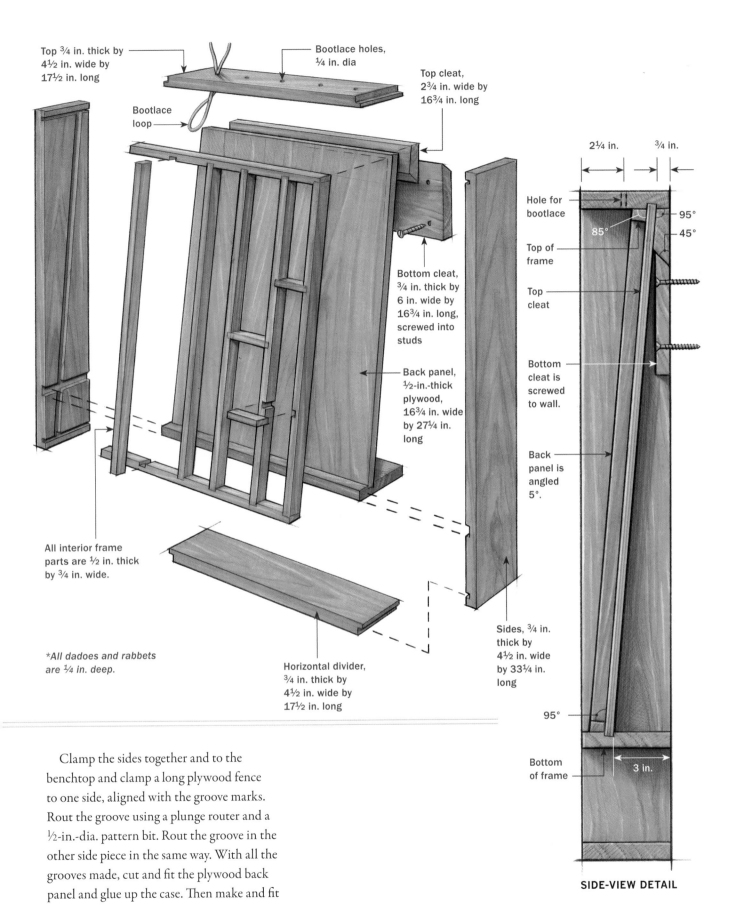

Top ¾ in. thick by 4½ in. wide by 17½ in. long

Bootlace loop

Bootlace holes, ¼ in. dia

Top cleat, 2¾ in. wide by 16¾ in. long

Bottom cleat, ¾ in. thick by 6 in. wide by 16¾ in. long, screwed into studs

Back panel, ½-in.-thick plywood, 16¾ in. wide by 27¼ in. long

All interior frame parts are ½ in. thick by ¾ in. wide.

*All dadoes and rabbets are ¼ in. deep.

Horizontal divider, ¾ in. thick by 4½ in. wide by 17½ in. long

Sides, ¾ in. thick by 4½ in. wide by 33¼ in. long

2¼ in.   ¾ in.

Hole for bootlace

Top of frame

Top cleat

95°
85°
45°

Bottom cleat is screwed to wall.

Back panel is angled 5°.

95°

Bottom of frame

3 in.

SIDE-VIEW DETAIL

Clamp the sides together and to the benchtop and clamp a long plywood fence to one side, aligned with the groove marks. Rout the groove using a plunge router and a ½-in.-dia. pattern bit. Rout the groove in the other side piece in the same way. With all the grooves made, cut and fit the plywood back panel and glue up the case. Then make and fit

Angled cuts made easy

Cut the top and bottom grooves for the back panel with a tilted dado blade. Then use a plunge router and angled fence to make the grooves in the sides.

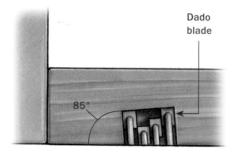

Dado blade

85°

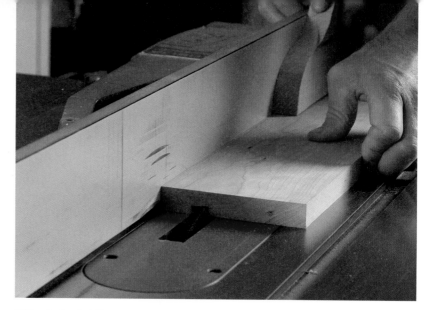

Tilt a dado. Cut the grooves in the top and the horizontal divider at 5°.

Layout blocks ensure that all the grooves meet. With the case dry-assembled, use offcuts from the back-panel stock to lay out the side grooves. Place these blocks in the top and bottom grooves and scribe around them with a knife.

Rout the sloping side grooves. Clamp a fence aligned with the scribe marks, and use a plunge router and ½-in. pattern bit.

the French cleat. Note how it is angled to sit flat against the back panel.

Cut and fit the interior frame

Start by making the top and bottom pieces of the frame. Cut them to length, then bevel one edge 5° so that the inward facing edge is at a right angle to the back panel (see drawing on p. 161). That means you bevel the top edge of the top piece and the bottom edge of the bottom piece.

Build the box first. The plywood back panel is glued into its grooves, making the cabinet rigid.

Glue in the interior frame. Install the top and bottom frame pieces first, then attach the vertical pieces. You can glue them to the back panel without clamps, but the joinery must be tight. Drill the bootlace holes in the short horizontal pieces before gluing them in.

Next, cut the dadoes for the vertical frame pieces in the top and bottom of the frame. Fit the vertical pieces, then cut the dadoes in them for the short horizontal frame pieces. After cutting and fitting the shorter pieces, drill ¼-in.-dia. holes in them for the lower bootlace hooks. Now glue the interior frame into the case. These tight-fitting parts require only spring clamps to hold them while the glue cures. After the interior frame has been installed, drill holes through the top of the case for the top bootlace hooks. Clamp a backer board to the opposite side to prevent tearout.

Finish the rack and tie up loose ends

I finished the rack with three coats of WATCO Danish Oil, which brings out the beauty of the wood, protects it from grime, and touches up easily if needed. Once the finish is dry, make the bootlace hooks. It will take some tries to get the right-length loop for each compartment. Don't get frustrated. As long as you can hook the knob of the plane through the loop and the plane sits in its compartment, you're good to go. Singe the ends of the loops to prevent fraying.

It won't take long to get the hang of this rack. Soon you'll be removing and replacing the planes with just one hand.

Holes for the hooks. Once the case is glued up, drill holes through the top piece for the bootlace hooks. Clamp a backer board underneath to prevent tearout.

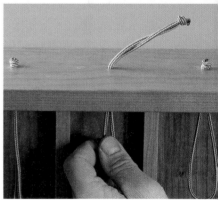

Custom hooks. Make a loop using a overhand knot (top) and thread it through its hole (above). Experiment to get the right-length loop for each plane.

BEFORE

AFTER

Divide and Conquer

MICHAEL PEKOVICH

he set of drawers in my workbench holds the tools I use most often, but until recently it didn't hold them very well.

I've always liked having the tools within reach, but I wasn't fond of the way they rattled and rolled around, threatening to damage one another. And I didn't enjoy having to rummage through a dusty jumble of stuff to find the tool I wanted.

I finally got tired of it and installed dividers. They are easy to cut and install, and they're adjustable. I didn't want to be locked into a layout that I might outgrow, so I used dividers that are dry-fit into dadoed end pieces. They fit securely, but can easily be removed and relocated as needed. Now, all my tools rest easy—and in plain sight. No more rattling, rolling, or rummaging.

Dado blade is the key to quick joinery

Use a dado set to make ¼-in.-wide test cuts in a scrap of wood. After thicknessing, rip all of your stock to fit the dadoes in the scrap piece. As one dado gets worn, move on to a fresh one. Leave the pieces long at this point.

For layout, simply arrange the tools in the drawer the way you want them. Then fit crosspieces to the drawer and mark them for

Get your stock ready. Use a dado set to make ¼-in.-wide test cuts in a piece of scrap. After thicknessing, rip all of your stock (top) to fit the dadoes in the scrap piece (above).

Dado both ends at the same time. To ensure that the carving-gouge dividers would line up, Pekovich dadoed both crosspieces together.

Don't bother with a drawing. Arrange the tools in the drawer the way you want them (top). Then fit crosspieces to the drawer and mark them for the dadoes (above).

the dadoes. For the carving-gouge dividers, I dadoed both crosspieces together to ensure that they would line up.

A layer of rubber mesh drawer liner cushions the tools and helps keep them from sliding. After marking and cutting the pieces to length, profile the dividers as needed for easy access to the tools and slide them into place.

Finishing touches. After marking and cutting the pieces to length (left), profile the dividers as needed and slide them into place (below).

Lumber Storage Solutions

ANDY BEASLEY

I once read that the idea of infinite space was perhaps the most difficult concept for the mind of man to grasp. I beg to differ. Anyone who ever has tried to create a functional shop knows that fitting it into a finite space is a far more challenging proposition. Once all of the necessary tools, materials, and that last bottle of glue have been shoehorned into the workshop, you can find yourself on the outside looking in.

When building my shop several years ago, I experimented with different layouts until I found the one that worked best for me. I've been happy with the result, largely because the lumber-storage system I developed added considerably to the efficiency of my shop while taking up little of its finite space.

Wall rack handles the long stuff

The centerpiece of my storage system is a horizontal rack along one wall. The rack is exceptionally stable, and the various levels hold a lot of material within a small footprint. The design is straightforward, the materials are relatively inexpensive, and the construction time is short.

I frequently store 16-ft. lengths of molding, so I decided to install six vertical stanchions to provide the necessary horizontal space. The 2x6 studs in the shop wall are on 16-in. centers; I installed a stanchion on every other one, or 32 in. on center. These stanchions are merely lengths of 1x4 pine, glued and nailed to 2x4 spacers. The spacers add stiffness, create pockets for the support arms, and provide a solid attachment point for the lag screws that mount the assembly to the wall.

Although the stanchion assembly is simple to build, it helps to choose stock that is straight, without bow or twist. Gluing and nailing the pieces together on a level floor is an easy way to keep them true.

This rack is designed to support considerable weight if it is mounted securely to a sturdy wall. To attach the stanchions to the shop wall, I first marked the locations of the electrical wires in the wall so that I could give them a wide berth. Then I secured the stanchions with 6-in. lag screws through the spacer blocks and into the wall studs.

This rack can be attached equally well to a concrete wall as long as heavy-duty masonry anchors are used. The small, plastic expanding anchors used to hang pictures on cinderblock walls won't provide the necessary pull-out resistance. For similar reasons, don't mount this rack to a hollow gypsum or paneled wall.

The head and foot of each stanchion help prevent twisting, stabilizing the rack when it's under load. The head is screwed to a ceiling truss, while the matching foot is glued securely to the floor.

Lumber at the ready. A wall-mounted rack keeps lumber organized and accessible without taking up valuable floor space.

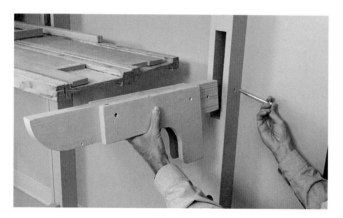

Simple mounting system. Lumber rests on a series of support arms that are bolted to stanchions.

The horizontal support arms do the hard work. They're made of 2x4s with ¾-in.-thick plywood gussets screwed to each side. I angled the arms upward 2° to keep material from sliding off, and I rounded the protruding ends to soften any inadvertent collision between my head and one of the arms. My wife painted most of the rack before installation. However, to prevent lumber from pick-ing up unwanted stains, the top edge of each arm was left unpainted.

I started at the top row and installed each arm by drilling a hole through the stanchions and the inner end of the arm. A ½-in.-dia., 4-in.-long bolt secures each arm. In the future, though, should I decide to change the eleva-tion of the arms, the oversize pockets in the stanchions give me the ability to drill a new bolt hole and shift each arm to a new location.

Roll-around cart for short pieces

Besides death, taxes, and slivers, I think the accumulation of lumber offcuts is about the only thing woodworkers can take for granted. The woodstove can handle just so much, and besides, that peanut-size chunk of walnut may come in handy someday. Owning up to my pack-rat tendencies, I built three storage carts for offcuts that fit in the unused area under the bottom shelf of the wall rack. I left the rest of that area open for future storage needs.

Wall rack for lumber

With stanchions spaced 32 in. on center, the rack can be made to fit a wall of any length and height.

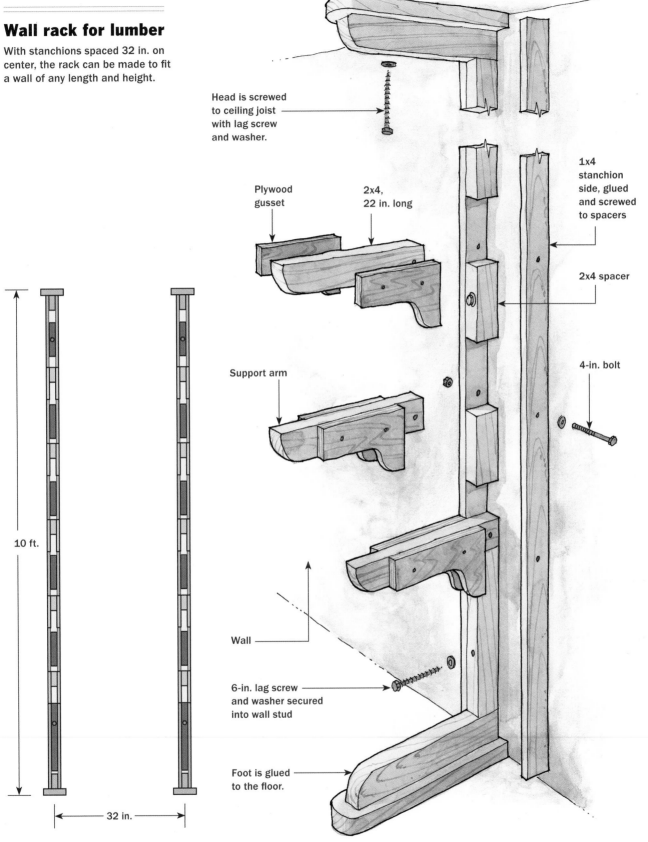

Head is screwed to ceiling joist with lag screw and washer.

Plywood gusset

2x4, 22 in. long

1x4 stanchion side, glued and screwed to spacers

2x4 spacer

Support arm

4-in. bolt

Wall

6-in. lag screw and washer secured into wall stud

Foot is glued to the floor.

10 ft.

32 in.

Rolling cart adds convenience. A framed plywood box on wheels provides the perfect place to store offcuts.

Cart for lumber offcuts

Simplified frame-and-panel construction means the cart assembles without much fuss, yet has plenty of strength.

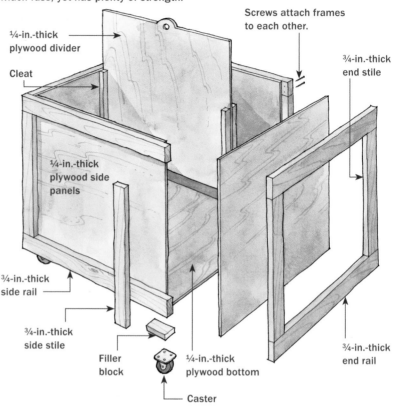

¼-in.-thick plywood divider

Cleat

¼-in.-thick plywood side panels

¾-in.-thick side rail

¾-in.-thick side stile

Filler block

¼-in.-thick plywood bottom

Caster

Screws attach frames to each other.

¾-in.-thick end stile

¾-in.-thick end rail

The carts are simple boxes on casters. To stave off the chaos that would ensue if I just threw scrap into the carts, I installed removable dividers, which allow for a rough sort of organization. By adding a removable plywood top to one of the carts, I immediately had a mobile workbench.

Vertical box stores sheet goods in minimal space

I'd initially planned to store sheet goods flat or on some sort of horizontal cart, but I discarded those ideas because they ate up too much floor space. The obvious answer was vertical storage. Holding 15 to 20 sheets, the rack I constructed is little more than a doubled-up plywood bottom, a few 2x4 posts, and a plywood top.

Because there's little outward pressure on this type of rack, it can be attached to a wall with either nails or wood screws. To this simple structure, I added a few user-friendly features. The 2x4 spacers on the side walls of the rack give me some finger room when I want to withdraw a sheet that's located near the edge. A layer of Plexiglas® covering the plywood bottom makes sliding even the heaviest sheet a breeze. And because I don't relish the idea of dinging the corner of an expensive sheet, I installed a pull-out pad to protect the pivoting corner as I load or unload material. To squeeze the last bit of utility from the rack, I use the outer frame as a place to hang levels, squares, and cutting jigs.

Choose and use. This vertical rack makes it easy to flip through the sheets and pull one out without damaging it.

Protective pad. The outside bottom corner of sheet goods gets some protection from damage, thanks to a pull-out pad.

A storage system works only if you use it

Just as a closet won't pick up that shirt you've thrown over a chair, a lumber rack won't do you any good if you don't use it. I've developed habits to keep the shop both uncluttered and efficient. At the end of each day, I select the offcuts I intend to keep. Any boards shorter than 24 in. go into the roll-around lumber cart; longer pieces are stored on the horizontal rack. I used to put these leftovers anywhere, but each time I brought in a new load of boards, I had too many little things to rearrange before I could place the incoming material on the rack.

When I return plywood or sheet goods to the vertical rack, I always write the new width on the exposed edge. That prevents miscalculations when I'm reviewing the material I have on hand for a project, and I don't have to slide out a piece to check its width.

This storage system works exceptionally well. Now, when work is going smoothly and all my materials are stowed neatly away, I sometimes let my mind wander to those minor problems of infinity.

Rack for sheet goods

Stored vertically in this rack, sheet goods like plywood and medium-density fiberboard (MDF) can be accessed with relative ease.

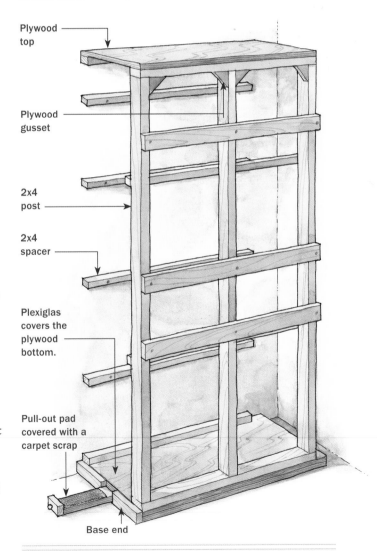

Plywood top

Plywood gusset

2x4 post

2x4 spacer

Plexiglas covers the plywood bottom.

Pull-out pad covered with a carpet scrap

Base end

Fire Safety in the Shop

BRUCE RYDEN

No matter the size of your shop, fire hazards are present day in and day out. Wood is a combustible material, but when it's in the form of a solid mass, such as a plank of lumber, it is difficult to ignite and to keep burning. Try holding a match to a large piece of wood and see which gets burned first, the wood or your fingers. If you took that same piece of wood, put it through a thickness planer, and held a match to the pile of shavings, you'd be amazed by how quickly it would ignite.

The best way to prevent a fire in your shop is to practice good housekeeping. Sawdust and wood shavings are the two most commonly dangerous products in a woodshop. They are ignited easily, and the fire can spread with unbelievable speed and intensity. The careless use, storage, and disposal of finishing supplies also are frequently encountered fire hazards. Many woodworkers store cans of varnish, containers of solvents and thinners, and organic-based finishes, such as linseed oil and tung oil, on open shelves in the shop, where they can provide the fuel to greatly accelerate the spread of a fire.

Prevention is mostly common sense

Three elements are required to cause a fire: fuel, oxygen, and a source of heat. Take away any one of them, and you cannot have combustion.

We need the oxygen to breathe, so we can't remove that. We often can remove the heat to prevent a fire (by not smoking or not using torches or welding equipment in a woodshop). But the easiest item to remove is the fuel. It may seem like a real chore to sweep up a pile of wood chips or shavings after a long day working in the shop, but by cleaning up, you can remove the most manageable portion of the three elements needed to start a fire.

Electricity, another hazard in most shops, often is blamed as the cause of a fire, but seldom is that borne out by a competent fire investigation. In a clean shop, this heat source rarely is the cause of a fire. If an electrical short circuit does occur, it must have a fuel to feed upon. Without contact with piles of sawdust or wood shavings, the likelihood of a short circuit starting a shop fire is

It could have been worse. Ellis Walentine, host of www.woodcentral.com, lost his entire shop in rural Pennsylvania in May 1999 to a fire; no one was hurt in the conflagration. He suspects the fire was caused when arcing in a loose connection in the electrical panel ignited some accumulated sawdust.

Store flammable liquids. A storage cabinet for flammable liquids is meant to keep a fire from getting much worse very quickly. Whether you buy one or build your own (on the facing page), it should have a self-closing door and a lip on the shelves to keep spilled liquids from escaping.

Dispose of oily rags. Rags soaked with flammable finishes can ignite spontaneously, so they must be disposed of properly. With its spring-loaded, self-closing lid, this red bucket prevents spontaneous combustion. A plastic bucket half-filled with water also will work.

improbable (but possible—see p. 175). Any tool or piece of machinery that has a cord that is frayed, cracked, or not in great condition should be replaced, and all electrical connections should be secured tightly.

One of the frequently forgotten and least understood causes of fire in the shop is spontaneous combustion of rags and waste. When an organic oil, such as linseed oil or tung oil, is applied to rags used for finishing, a heating process takes place. This heating takes place only in the presence of oxygen, and when the heat given off by the process is not allowed to dissipate, it will continue to rise until the rags reach a temperature that is high enough to ignite them.

By placing used rags in a steel container with water and a cover on it, this process will not occur. An acceptable alternative is to hang the rags in a single layer on a clothesline or a fence, which allows the rags to dry without the heat buildup.

The application of a flammable finish by hand is not without hazards, but if there is good air exchange with fresh outside air, the vapors given off by the finish can be diluted to a safe level. Most of these vapors are heavier than air and will sink to the floor. Be especially careful about any possible source of ignition (such as water heaters, furnaces, portable heaters, and electric fans) down near the floor close to where you are working.

The proper storage of flammable and combustible materials used in finishing projects is one of the most neglected safety issues in many workshops. Cans and sometimes even glass bottles stored on open shelves can fall off and release large quantities of hazardous materials. Spray cans containing any flammable or combustible materials are extremely dangerous items to have sitting

Construction detail

The 2x4 frame serves as a spill-proof lip on the front of the shelf. The two layers of drywall greatly increase the time that it would take a fire to ignite the liquids in the cabinet.

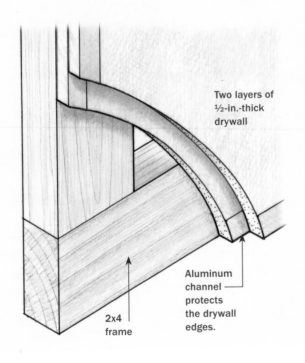

Two layers of ½-in.-thick drywall

Aluminum channel protects the drywall edges.

2x4 frame

A shop-built solution to storing flammable liquids. Ryden built a basic storage cabinet for flammables in the garage adjacent to his shop. He used 2x4s for the frame and covered that with two layers of drywall. He encased the edges of the drywall with aluminum channel to keep the gypsum from crumbling. By hinging the door at the top, it self-closes when he removes the strut that holds the door open so he can access the shelf inside.

on open shelves. These cans are considered by the National Fire Protection Association as the most hazardous of all flammable or combustible materials. Once ignited, finish supplies quickly can turn a small fire into a dangerous, raging inferno.

Commercially available storage cabinets for finishes can be expensive. But for small home shops, you can make your own inexpensive version by surrounding the contents on all sides with two layers of ½-in.-thick drywall, which will greatly slow the speed at which a fire will spread to the finishes inside the cabinet. The door should be self-closing, and the shelves should be lipped to contain any spilled liquid.

Combating a fire in the shop. If a fire occurs, damage will be minimized if a sprinkler system has been installed. Heat detectors provide an early warning and don't commonly suffer malfunctions in dusty environments. A fire extinguisher can prevent a small fire from getting worse, but you should always call the fire department first.

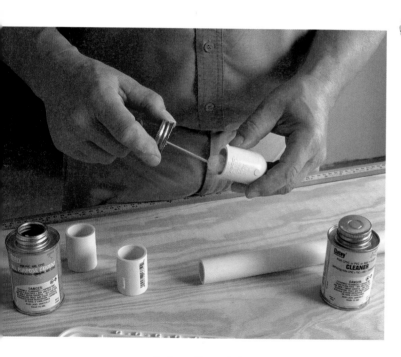

Automatic sprinkler system. A typical sprinkler head will spray an area about 10 ft. by 10 ft. You can connect sprinklers to copper, galvanized, or PVC plastic pipes. PVC is the least expensive to install. Prime the pieces first with a cleaner, then daub on the cement.

Heat detector. Smoke detectors can malfunction because of the dust found in the air of most woodshops. Heat detectors are a better choice in dusty environments. They are activated when the room temperature reaches a preset level, usually 135°F to 165°F. The heat detector in Ryden's shop is powered by a circuit from the electrical service panel, and it is connected to a commercial alarm service through a telephone line.

Fire extinguisher. Use an extinguisher rated ABC to fight woodshop fires fueled by wood, finishing supplies, or bad electrical connections. Extinguishers should always be placed near an exit so you won't get trapped by a fire while trying to access the extinguisher.

Equip the shop with heat detectors

The most sensitive detection device is the human nose, which can smell smoke long before any electronic gadget can detect it. But when you're not in the shop, you must rely on other detection devices. Electronic detectors fall into three major categories: heat, smoke, and flames. Of these, heat detectors are best for a woodworking shop. Smoke-detection devices—both the ionization type and the photoelectric type—are susceptible to false alarms caused by the dust generated in a woodshop. Flame detectors are not as susceptible to dust contamination, but they are much more expensive than heat detectors.

There are three types of heat detectors: fixed temperature, rate of rise, and a combination of both types. The fixed-temperature devices usually are set in the 135°F to 165°F range. When the temperature of the room reaches the preset level, the alarm sounds. The rate-of-rise detectors measure how quickly the room temperature increases. When it rises more than a certain number of degrees in a preset time period, the alarm sounds. The combination-type detector is the best for woodworking shops because it will sound the alarm as soon as it detects either a slow, smoldering fire or a quickly spreading fire. This alarm can be either a local alarm (sounding just inside or outside of the shop), or you can connect it to a monitored service (such as ADT or Brinks).

Putting out a fire once it starts

While detection devices are good to have in the shop, they do nothing to slow or stop the spread of a fire. This is best done by an automatic sprinkler system that utilizes water to be discharged only in the vicinity of the fire, most often extinguishing the fire before it can spread. Most of us would rather come into the shop and find some water damage than find that the entire shop has been destroyed. There are systems that can be installed to detect water flowing through the sprinkler piping and sound an alarm, thereby reducing the water damage.

Sprinkler heads are readily available and inexpensive. It only took me eight hours to plumb my 900-sq.-ft. shop with sprinklers — a small investment for a lot of peace of mind.

The most common sprinkler heads are the pendant style, which hang below the piping, and the upright style, which stand above the piping. They must be installed in the correct position or they will not function properly. In most shop situations, the pendant head is appropriate. These heads are available from local fire-sprinkler contractors, but there are also some online suppliers. The only application where water-sprinkler heads are not appropriate is in an unheated shop in a cold climate.

Place extinguishers near an exit

Every shop should have at least one well-maintained, easily accessible, portable fire extinguisher. Fire extinguishers are first-aid appliances. You must know when to use them and when to back off and let a professional handle the situation. The first thing you should do when a fire is detected is to call the fire department. They can always go home if they're not needed.

Fires are classified into four different categories: A, B, C, and D. The easiest way I know to remember them is as follows:

Category A involves anything that leaves ash when it burns (paper, wood, cloth); category B involves burning liquid (gasoline, paint, paint thinners, oil-based products); category C includes circuit fires (live electrical fires in wiring, wiring devices, motors, electrical appliances); and category D fires involve combustible metals, which usually are not found in woodworking shops.

The most effective fire extinguisher for a shop is at least a 10-lb. multipurpose dry-chemical fire extinguisher, rated ABC on the label. This type of extinguisher can be applied to any kind of fire in a shop, has sufficient agent to extinguish almost any fire in its early stage, and can be used with minimal training.

Another consideration with fire extinguishers is where to place them. You should always have to go toward an exit door to access the extinguisher. That way, if the fire suddenly builds, you have a way out of the shop without having to go past the fire. Always keep a door at your back when using a fire extinguisher. Never allow a fire to come between you and a safe way out.

Sources

SPRINKLERS
Sprinkler heads can be purchased from either a sprinkler-installation contractor or a plumbing-supply store.

HEAT DETECTORS
Heat detectors are offered at most electrical-supply stores and at many online suppliers.

FIRE EXTINGUISHERS
Fire extinguishers are available at most hardware stores and home centers.

Cutting-Edge First Aid

PATRICK SULLIVAN

Woodworkers spend a lifetime handling razor-sharp tools, power equipment with exposed blades, and boards that harbor splinters and fasteners. In this environment, there's always the risk of an injury.

Usually woodworkers cut their fingers and occasionally the palms of their hands. Although the hand often will recover from minor injuries even if it receives no care at all, recovery is faster with less scarring and less risk of infection if it's treated properly. For more serious cuts and eye injuries, however, what you do first can have an impact on the rest of your life.

As a woodworker and physician, I understand the types of injuries that are common in the shop, and I know how they should be treated. Forget the first-aid kits offered in drug stores. Forget much of the misguided advice found in popular manuals. The woodworking environment is unique, and I'll tell you about some specialized equipment and supplies that work well there. I'll also show you a few tricks on treating wounds—from stopping bleeding to cleaning to bandaging—based on proven medical principles. In the end, you'll learn how to treat injuries in a way that gets you back to work as soon as possible.

How to handle most cuts

The enemy of healing is infection. The germs that live on lumber and tools generally do not cause disease; essentially, all the risk is from bacteria you already carry on your skin. A wound allows those skin germs to reach the more vulnerable tissue beneath the skin. The problem gets worse if there is dirt, sawdust, debris, or dead tissue in the wound.

Soap and water

The most effective treatment for all wounds is immediate washing with soap and clean water. (You can skip this if you need to go to the emergency room, because they will clean the wound there.) Washing drastically reduces the number of germs and takes away dirt and debris in which bacteria can hide and multiply.

I have seen several Internet pictures and videos that show first-aid techniques that advocate wiping the wound clean with a damp paper towel or gauze pad. This is the most ineffective way to wash a wound.

The surest way to clean a wound is to hold the cut under running water for several minutes and lather thoroughly. If soap is not available, plain water will do a credible job. Wash every wound, whether you can see contamination or not. Waterless hand cleaners and antiseptic solutions may be better than nothing, but they are not a proven substitute for washing. If you can wash effectively, you do not need these products.

Doctors and first-aid manuals in the past have routinely recommended the use of

Lather up

Wash both hands vigorously enough to generate lots of lather under a strong stream of warm running water for several minutes. While washing, hold the cut open and flush the wound for at least a minute. Ignore any bleeding this may cause. Dry both hands on a clean paper towel.

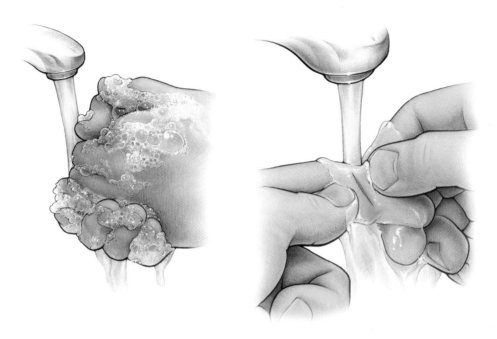

an antibiotic ointment, but recent surgical research proves that clean wounds need no antibiotic if they are washed well and closed promptly. Moreover, the ointment preparation discourages the formation of a scab, which is the most effective wound closure available. Skip any antibiotic ointment unless dirt and debris were driven into the wound and cannot be washed out.

Five minutes of pressure

After washing the wound, you need to stop the bleeding. Apply pressure directly over the wound for five minutes without interruption to help form a clot. If you peek, the clock starts all over again.

TIP If you get a minor cut, say, while you're in the middle of a glue-up, you don't have to stop working. Put on an examination glove, and wrap masking tape snugly around the finger directly over the cut. The glove keeps blood off the woodwork, and pressure from the tape will usually stop the bleeding in 5 to 10 minutes. After removing the tape and glove, wash your hands thoroughly, and close and dress the wound.

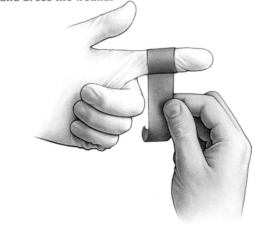

Build a custom kit

A first-aid kit for woodworkers looks very different from the kits sold in drugstores. It contains materials for closing cuts, flexible coverings for wounds, tools for removing splinters, and eye wash. Many of these products are available from multiple manufacturers.

1. Coban tape
2. Glue syringe
3. Eye wash
4. Tegaderm bandages
5. Band-Aids
6. Examination gloves
7. Magnifying lens
8. Steri-Strips
9. X-Acto knife
10. Krazy® Glue
11. Scissors
12. Tape
13. Tweezers

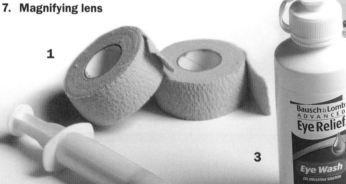

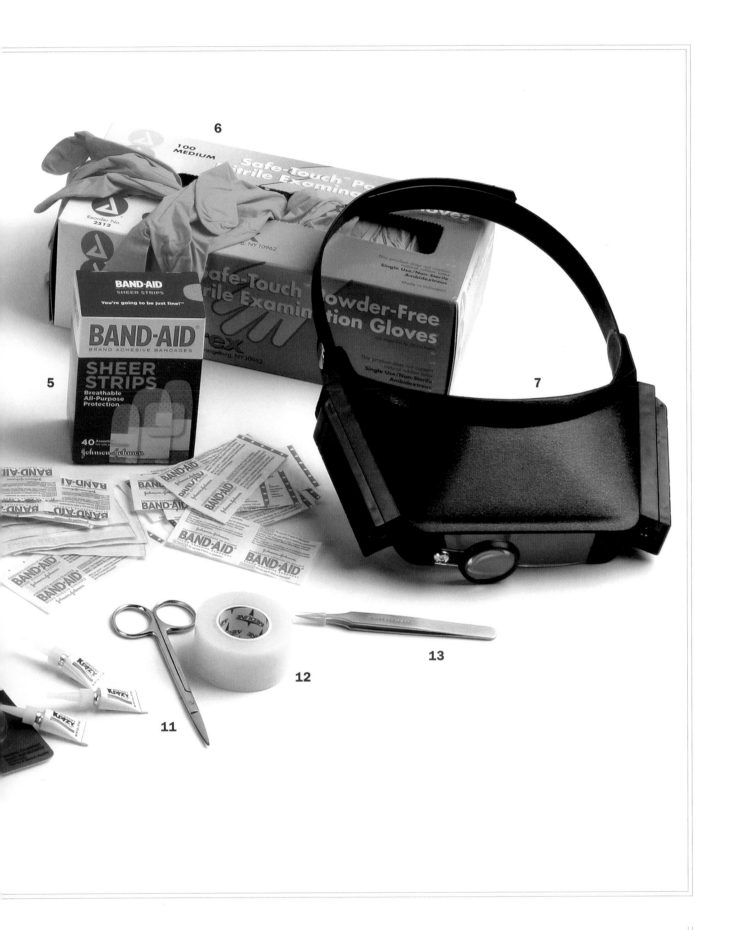

Be direct

Don't be afraid to touch the cut. Apply pressure directly over the wound (bottom), not below it (top).

Wrong

Right

Adhesive-backed Steri-Strips keep cuts closed

Dry the skin around the wound, then cut the strips to length. Remove the paper backing and apply. Adhere the strip to one side of the cut, push the wound edges together so they just meet, and stick the strip down on the other side.

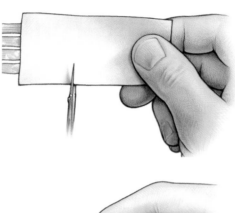

Close the wound before bandaging

When you get cut, keeping the two edges of the wound firmly closed will help it heal rapidly. Cuts from sharp tools penetrate cleanly, which makes them easier to close and faster to heal. Wounds with frayed or crushed edges (such as those made by a spinning tool) take a bit longer to heal. In either case, you want to wash and close the wound to pull the sliced skin back together.

Standard adhesive bandages cover the wound but don't securely close it. As soon as you start using your hands, skin movement will reopen the cut. Hospitals often use a specialized tape product called Steri-Strip™, which you can buy without a prescription in most drugstores or online.

It is also possible to glue wounds closed with ordinary cyanoacrylate glue. Both methods work better if you have a helper to either hold the wound closed or to apply the Steri-Strips or glue.

A different kind of glue-up

Cyanoacrylate glue works for closing a wound. But the job is not like butting two boards together. Do not apply glue inside the wound. Instead, push the skin edges together and spread a thin layer of glue across the top of the skin, interrupting the glue at short intervals to preserve flexibility. Don't use the activator spray that comes with some glues.

Wrong   Right

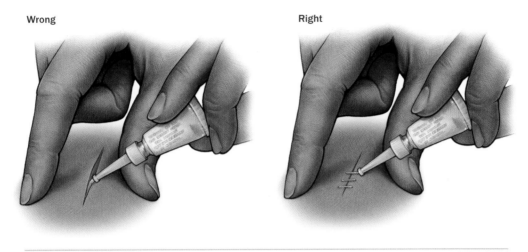

Better than a Band-Aid®

After closing the wound with a Steri-Strip, apply a Tegaderm bandage. Put on the bandage and then peel off the paper frame. If you need to cut the bandage to a smaller size, do it while all the backing paper is still in place. The bandage is thin and flexible, allowing nearly full knuckle movement.

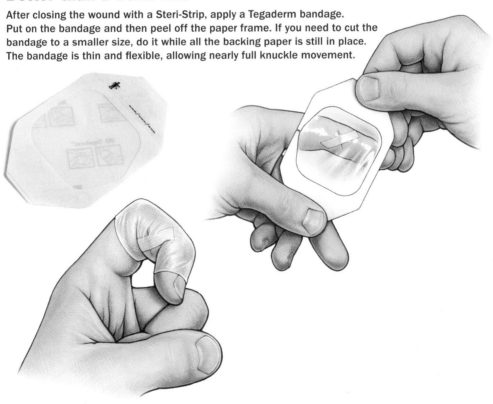

Smarter bandages

If you go to an emergency room with a hand injury, you'll come home with a huge, fluffy bandage that will attract a lot of sympathy but render you unable to work. Emergency rooms use gauze as the main element of bandaging. Gauze is light as air, extremely flexible, and breathes like it wasn't there at all. However, you cannot work wood while wearing gauze.

Woodworkers need bandages that are flexible, thin, and tough. It is also convenient to have bandages that shed water, sawdust, and glue, and yet breathe so the skin stays dry. Here are two bandages that you can use after you've closed the wound or after you've come home from the ER.

The first option is to cover the area with a Tegaderm™ dressing (see bottom drawing on p. 187). Tegaderm is a transparent medical dressing (made by 3M™) that's flexible, tough, and stretchy. It is great for hand wounds because it can be conformed to a number of shapes and is so smooth that it won't catch on any sharp edges, like an adhesive bandage can. This product is available with and without a nonstick, absorbent pad in the center. Many wounds will seep a small amount of serum in the first few hours after bandaging, and the absorbent pads are useful then. Later, they may be unnecessary.

This might be all you need. If you have to handle rough lumber, or do work that applies a lot of friction or abrasion to your hands, consider wearing leather or fabric gloves to protect the dressing.

Injuries that involve the palm or the webs between the fingers are very hard to bandage.

When you need more holding power, use Coban tape

It's hard to keep a bandage in place on the palm of your hand, so wrap the dressing with Coban tape (1 in. wide usually is sufficient). First take a couple of wraps around the wrist. This serves to anchor the whole bandage. Then continue with several wraps around the palm. End the Coban on the back of the hand or wrist, where it will receive the least rubbing.

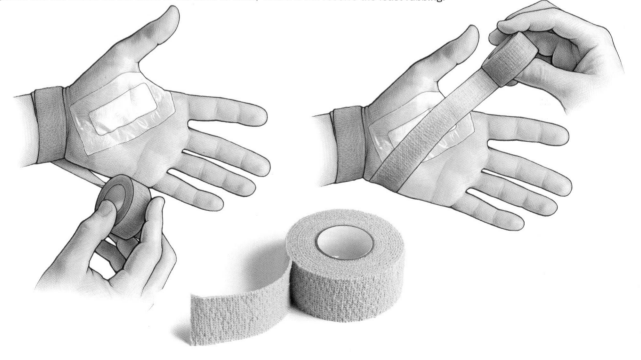

Deep cleaning

As you wash, open the wound as much as possible, and squirt water in with a squeeze bottle or a glue syringe. Don't be bashful about the amount of water. You want to flush the wound vigorously enough to get rid of any debris at the bottom of the puncture.

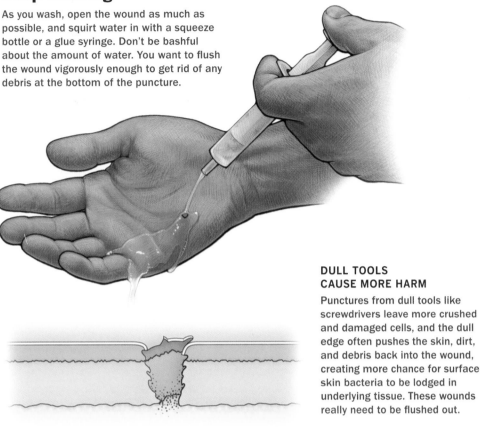

DULL TOOLS CAUSE MORE HARM

Punctures from dull tools like screwdrivers leave more crushed and damaged cells, and the dull edge often pushes the skin, dirt, and debris back into the wound, creating more chance for surface skin bacteria to be lodged in underlying tissue. These wounds really need to be flushed out.

For these areas, cover the closed wound with Tegaderm, and then wrap Coban™ around the hand as necessary. Coban is a very stretchy bandage that sticks to itself, but not to anything else. It is excellent for bandages involving the palm or wrist because it stretches greatly but always remains snug.

Punctures: Wash away debris

Punctures from clean, sharp tools like narrow chisels, scratch awls, and marking knives should pose very little hazard and require very little treatment (unless they penetrate into joints or cut tendons). The wounds tend to close themselves. Wash thoroughly and apply a small bandage until bleeding stops.

If you have a puncture wound caused by a dull tool, you have an increased chance of infection (see drawing above). First wash the area thoroughly. As you wash, flush out the wound with water using a squeeze bottle or glue syringe. Apply Tegaderm with an absorbent pad. If the wound becomes more puffy and painful over a period of several days, have it seen by a doctor.

Puncture wounds carry a very small risk of tetanus. You were immunized against tetanus in childhood, but your immunity needs a booster every 10 years. Keep this up to date.

Do you need a doctor?

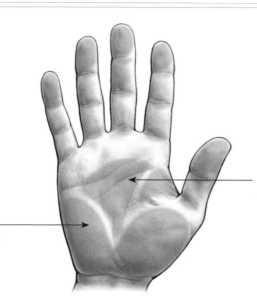

VULNERABLE AREAS OF THE HAND

Areas highlighted in green contain very few vulnerable structures, such as tendons. Unless the wound obviously penetrates into a bone or joint, cuts here typically can be treated easily at home.

Areas in red, however, contain tendons. Deep cuts in these areas are likely to have damaged the tendons or tendon sheaths and should be examined by a doctor.

IF THE CUT WON'T CLOSE, GET IT STITCHED

Cuts that do not slice all the way through don't require stitches because the lower layer of skin keeps the wound reasonably closed.

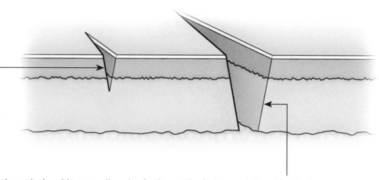

The cut on the right penetrates all the way through the skin, revealing the fat beneath. A deep cut like this that's under 1 in. long usually can be treated at home; if it's longer than 2 in., the wound needs to be stitched. In between 1 in. and 2 in., the decision to get stitched depends on the location of the wound (below).

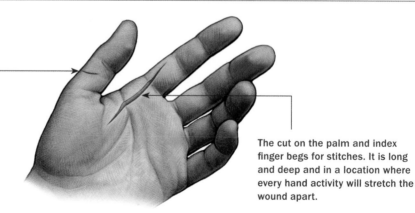

The cut on the thumb can be treated at home. It is short, and although deep, tends to close itself. Normal hand movements will not apply stress to the wound.

The cut on the palm and index finger begs for stitches. It is long and deep and in a location where every hand activity will stretch the wound apart.

Stubborn splinters need to be sliced out

To reach long slivers that tunnel through the skin, use an X-Acto knife with a No. 11 blade. First wash your hand and the blade. Insert the back of the blade along the top of the splinter, and gently slice open the skin with the tip of the blade. Slice along the splinter's length to expose it as much as possible, then pull it out with tweezers.

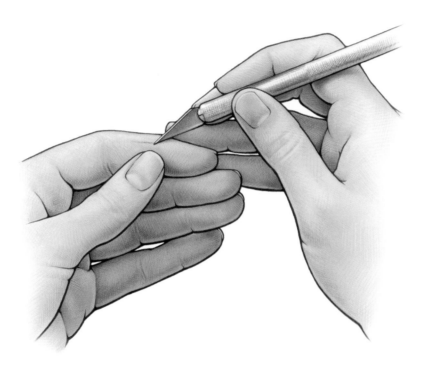

Splinters: Pull or slice them out

Everyone who works with wood has had splinters in their skin, and virtually everyone has struggled to remove them. If you have trouble seeing the splinter, use magnifying glasses, whether it's a pair of inexpensive reading glasses or visor-type magnifiers that you can wear over eyeglasses. These magnifiers may come in handy for other shop uses, too, like working with small parts or chiseling to a line in tight spaces between dovetails.

Usually you can pull out the splinter with a pair of tweezers. However, if a splinter has tunneled a long distance under your skin, you'll have to gently slice the skin to reach it using a No. 11 blade in either a disposable scalpel or an X-Acto® knife. After slicing, pull out the splinter with tweezers.

Be sure to wash your hands and the blade thoroughly before you probe around in the

Rinse and repeat

The safest and easiest way to remove foreign particles in the eye is to rinse them away with a spray of eye wash. Lift the eyelid and spray vigorously. If necessary, repeat several times.

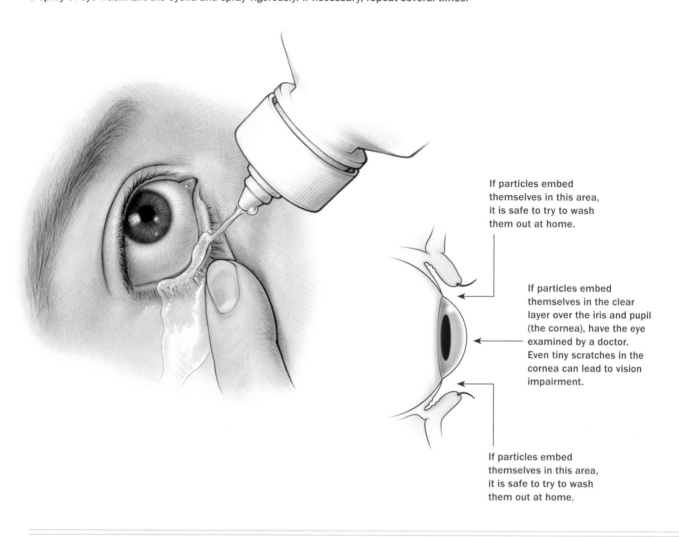

If particles embed themselves in this area, it is safe to try to wash them out at home.

If particles embed themselves in the clear layer over the iris and pupil (the cornea), have the eye examined by a doctor. Even tiny scratches in the cornea can lead to vision impairment.

If particles embed themselves in this area, it is safe to try to wash them out at home.

skin. Sterility is not necessary, but cleanliness is very important. Usually no dressing is needed; but if you had to dig so deeply that the wound bleeds significantly, then dress this as you would a cut.

Eyes: Rinse carefully or see a doctor

When you cut wood, especially with a router or tablesaw, sawdust (and sometimes other material) will fly. If some of that small debris ends up in your eye, your natural tears will usually wash it away. If the debris digs in and resists being washed away by tears, the best answer is to retract the eyelid away from the eyeball, and flush the eye with an eye-wash solution.

Get someone to help you. Lie on your back—it is hard to flood the eye with solution while you are upright. Have your helper put on your magnifiers and look in your eye for the debris. Regardless of whether they see the offending particle or not, have them squirt the solution under both lids. Use

Serious injury? What to do as you head to the hospital.

Some woodworking injuries demand professional care. Cuts that are deep enough to obviously penetrate into joints or bone, or that appear to cut tendons, should be treated by a doctor within a couple of hours. These injuries require the removal of foreign material embedded at the bottom of the wound and may require special suturing. They also carry greater risks of infection, and preventive antibiotic treatment is sometimes needed. For these wounds, stop the bleeding by applying pressure with a gauze pad or a clean paper towel and have someone drive you to the emergency room.

If you tangle with a power saw, that is going to mean a trip to the hospital. There is little that can or should be done in the shop, other than applying pressure to the wound and arranging for rapid transportation to the hospital. If you cut off some part of your hand, press directly on the wound to stop the bleeding, seal the amputated part in a zippered plastic bag, and get to the hospital fast. Don't try to drive yourself. If that trip is going to take more than an hour, carry the plastic bag in some ice or cold products from your freezer. Amputated fingers can survive for more than six hours.

Any kind of injury to the eyes is scary. Any injury that penetrates the eyeball or cuts through the eyelid must be seen by a specialist. If tiny flecks of wood or metal embed themselves in the cornea (the clear layer overlaying the iris and pupil), have them removed in the ER. When in doubt about any eye injury, you should have the eye examined by a pro. Tape a gauze pad or a tissue over the closed eye while you are on your way to the hospital. This discourages the eyelids from moving, which usually reduces any discomfort.

towels or tissues to sop up the excess, and use plenty of liquid. If that does not work, do it again. If repeated irrigation of the eye does not dislodge the particle, seek professional help. Never use tweezers or hard instruments in the area of the eye.

If there is so much spasm of the eyelids that you cannot open the eye enough to see what is going on, that suggests a more serious eye injury, and you should get immediate professional help.

Protect Yourself from Wood Dust

JEFF MILLER

Wood dust is a woodworker's constant companion and a constant threat. It doesn't take much airborne dust to exceed the exposure limits recommended by the National Institute for Occupational Safety and Health. In fact, you'll quickly blow past them when machining or sanding wood. Dust collectors and air cleaners help control wood dust, but even when optimized for your shop, they don't catch it all. The smallest and most dangerous particles escape them.

Exposure to those minute particles can cause nasal and sinus-cavity irritation, allergies, lung congestion, chronic cough, and cancer. That's why it's important to wear a dust mask or a powered respirator whenever you're producing dust or working in the shop afterward.

You're more likely to wear a dust mask or respirator if it's comfortable and fits well. You might need to look beyond your local hardware store, but great choices are out there. In fact, there are so many options you might feel overwhelmed. But that won't happen if you know how dust masks and respirators work, how to tell if one fits you well, and which features make one more comfortable.

I tested a large selection of masks and respirators and had the editors at *Fine Woodworking* do the same. I'll tell you what we liked about them and what we didn't.

That will help you know where to begin your search for a good-fitting and effective dust mask or respirator.

After all of our testing, it's clear that there are a few key features that make for a great mask or respirator. You should put them at the top of your list before you shop.

Filters for wood dust

For protection from wood dust, look for a mask rated N95, N99, or N100. The ratings don't apply to powered respirators, but all the respirators tested clean the air as well as an N95 mask does.

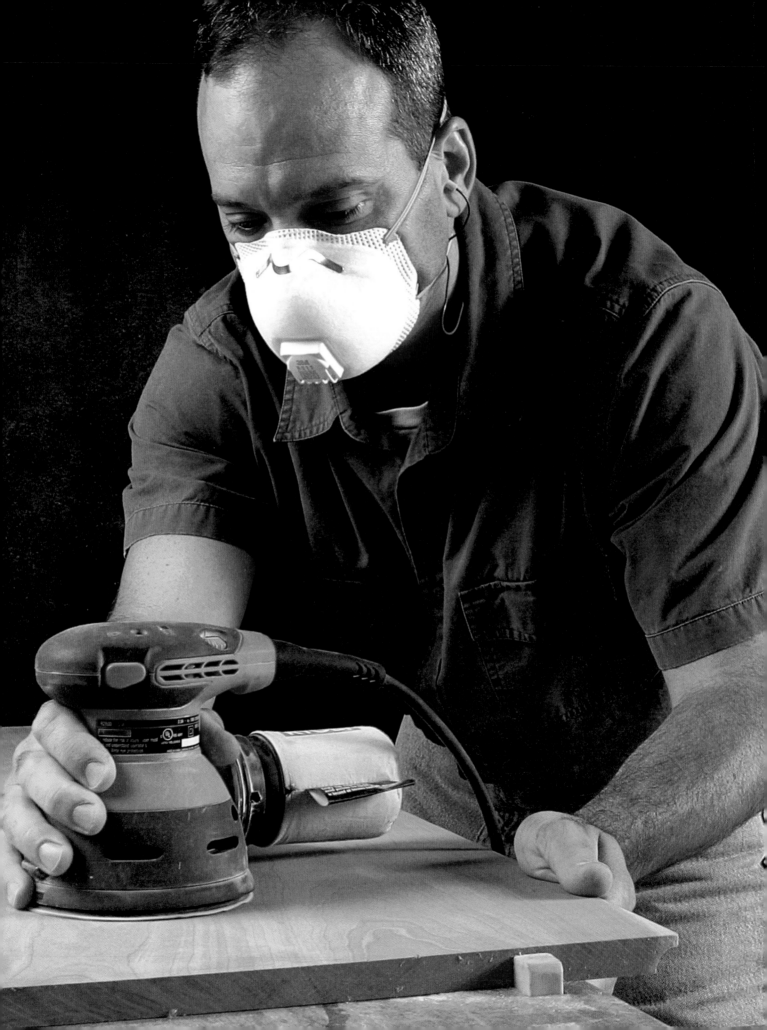

A place to hang your mask. The Moldex Handy Strap makes hanging a mask around your neck a snap (left), a big plus when you need to take it off momentarily to speak, get a drink, or make an adjustment. The strap makes putting the mask on easier, too (below).

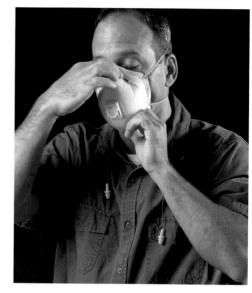

A better fit for more noses. Masks with adjustable nosepieces work for more people because they can be tailored to the individual's nose. The nosepieces help prevent fogging by giving a better seal around the nose.

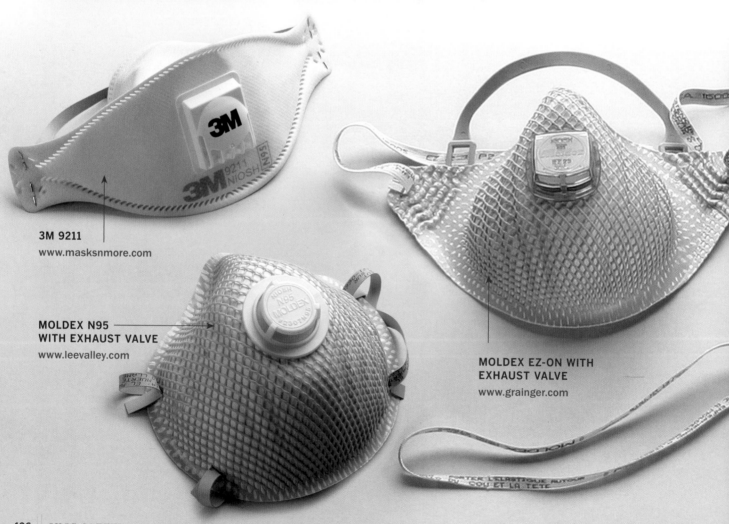

3M 9211
www.masksnmore.com

MOLDEX N95 WITH EXHAUST VALVE
www.leevalley.com

MOLDEX EZ-ON WITH EXHAUST VALVE
www.grainger.com

Comfort and fit matter most

An exhaust valve is an indispensable feature on a dust mask. In fact, we recommend you steer clear of any dust mask that doesn't have one. Exhaust valves clear the warm air you exhale, prevent safety glasses from fogging, and help keep your face cooler.

You also should look for a mask that is made from face-friendly material. The interior of the 3M 8511, for example, is soft and fleece-like. An adjustable nosepiece is important, because it allows the mask to form a tighter seal against your face and allows you to customize the mask to the shape of your nose.

Adjustable straps are a big plus, because they make for a tighter fit. Testers liked the adjustability of the straps on the Willson® Saf-T-Fit Plus and applauded the versatility

Get a Vent

Our testers clearly favored vented masks because they are more comfortable. They allow hot air to easily escape through the front of the mask, so your face stays cooler and your glasses won't fog.

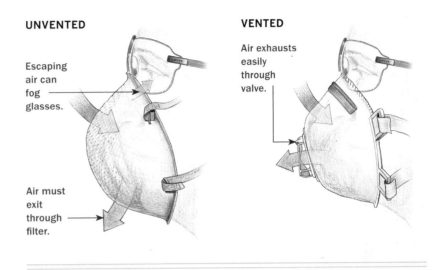

UNVENTED

Escaping air can fog glasses.

Air must exit through filter.

VENTED

Air exhausts easily through valve.

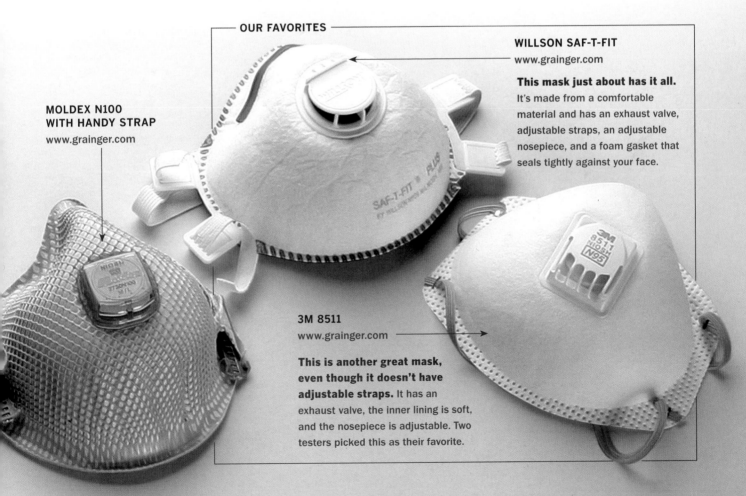

OUR FAVORITES

MOLDEX N100 WITH HANDY STRAP
www.grainger.com

WILLSON SAF-T-FIT
www.grainger.com

This mask just about has it all. It's made from a comfortable material and has an exhaust valve, adjustable straps, an adjustable nosepiece, and a foam gasket that seals tightly against your face.

3M 8511
www.grainger.com

This is another great mask, even though it doesn't have adjustable straps. It has an exhaust valve, the inner lining is soft, and the nosepiece is adjustable. Two testers picked this as their favorite.

Which one is right for you?

For most people, a high-quality dust mask works great. A powered respirator is a better choice if you need protection from flying chips or if you have facial hair, which keeps a dust mask from working properly. Most respirators have integrated, safety-rated face shields.

DUST MASKS REQUIRE A TIGHT FIT

A dust mask should seal tightly against your face. That keeps bad air from seeping in.

POWERED RESPIRATORS USE POSITIVE PRESSURE

Respirators use a fan to pull dirty air through a filter. The clean air flows down over the face, preventing bad air from flowing into the mask.

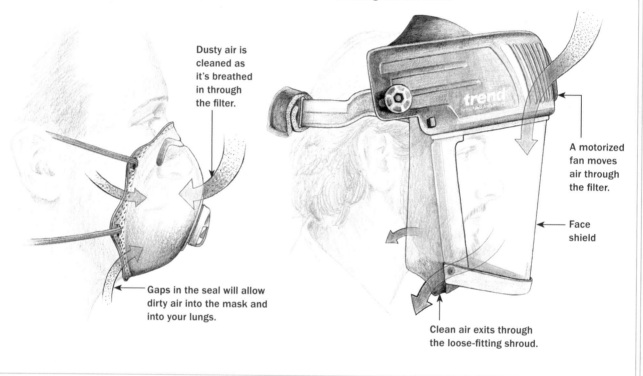

Dusty air is cleaned as it's breathed in through the filter.

Gaps in the seal will allow dirty air into the mask and into your lungs.

A motorized fan moves air through the filter.

Face shield

Clean air exits through the loose-fitting shroud.

of the Moldex® Handy Strap, which allows you to hang the mask comfortably around your neck.

Some features don't reveal themselves until you have a mask on. You don't want a mask that interferes with your vision or safety glasses, prevents you from speaking audibly, or interferes with hearing protection.

Because they have nearly all of these features, two masks really stood out from the rest: the 3M 8511 and the Willson Saf-T-Fit.

Respirators are harder to peg than dust masks, but there are a few key features to look for. The weight and balance of the helmet, for example, are important. If a respirator doesn't sit well on your head, you'll take it off

Protection from the big stuff, too. Many respirators have an integrated safety-rated face shield, which makes them great for turners.

Powered respirators

AIRCAP2
www.woodcraft.com

The filters and a fan are perched on the cap of this lightweight respirator. The face shield is not a safety device.

TRITON POWERED RESPIRATOR
www.woodcraft.com

In addition to being a respirator, the Triton provides a full-face shield, a helmet, and integral hearing protection. A Belt pack holds the fan, filter, and batteries. The fan and filter are connected to the helmet by a hose. It's great for rough work, but the face shield distorts your vision.

POWER AIR RESPIRATOR
www.rockler.com

This respirator resembles a reusable dust mask, but it's heavier because the filter, fan, and motor are on the mask. The batteries go in a belt pack. Everyone who tested this one found it uncomfortable.

OUR FAVORITES

TREND AIRSHIELD
www.envirosafetyproducts.com

Testers found the Airshield comfortable because of its padded headband. And even though the fan, motor, filter, and battery are perched on your brow, its weight is reasonably well balanced.

TREND AIRSHIELD PRO
www.envirosafetyproducts.com

The filter, fan, motor, and battery are located on the top of this respirator, so its weight is very well balanced. The optional earmuffs work well once you get everything adjusted. It provides the best filtration of all the powered respirators tested.

Reusable masks:
A good alternative for some

Disposable masks and those with replaceable filters clean air in the same way. The difference shows up when it's time to replace the filter. With a reusable mask, you replace just the filter section and keep the "frame" that holds it. Although they cost more up front, their filters last longer and are less expensive. They are heavier and can be less comfortable than disposables, but if you find one that fits you well, a reusable mask could be a good option.

NORTH CFR-1 COM-FIT
www.grainger.com

very quickly. And the face shield shouldn't distort or interfere with your vision. You also should be able to wear some kind of hearing protection with the respirator on.

Of the respirators we tested, the Trend® Airshield® and Airshield Pro distinguished themselves for comfort, clarity of vision, and overall user-friendliness.

Keep the clean air flowing

Dust masks don't last forever. Replace yours when it becomes difficult to breathe through, when the mask no longer seals properly, or when it is damaged.

If you use a respirator, make sure to check its airflow regularly. When it doesn't move enough clean air, it's time to replace the batteries, the filter, or both.

Sound Advice

DAVID HEIM

Hearing protectors are the workshop equivalent of the galoshes your mother nagged you to wear. If you obeyed your mother then, chances are you're pretty diligent now about using hearing protectors whenever you turn on noisy shop machines. But if you didn't listen to Mom, you probably forgo ear protectors, thinking they're too uncomfortable, you'll get used to the noise, or you needn't bother because you'll be working for only a few minutes. And you probably still wreck your dress shoes in the rain.

We posted a poll on www.FineWoodworking.com asking what type of hearing protection people used most often. More than 6 in 10 of the 1,018 respondents said they used earmuff-style protectors. Disposable foam plugs came in a distant second. But 1 in 10 said they usually don't wear hearing protection.

In fact, hearing protectors are as essential to a well-equipped, safe shop as good lighting, safety glasses, and an effective dust collector. Sounds that are too loud, even if they only last a short time, will damage your hearing. The louder the sound, the faster it can cause harm. And you don't get used to loudness—you lose your hearing and/or end up with tinnitus, a permanent ringing in the ears. The problem is that hearing damage builds up in tiny increments over the course of a lifetime, and before you know it, it's too late.

You probably need to wear hearing protectors more often than you think, but that no longer has to mean using plugs that seem as form-fitting as a tapered 2x4 or wearing muffs that make you feel as if you're in a soundproof room.

A wave of new technology

The simplest, least expensive earplugs and muffs reduce sound levels uniformly. They're designed to absorb some of the energy in the sound waves hitting our ears, cutting it by, say, 20 db. Many newer products are smarter, providing variable protection. Some plugs have pinholes that allow you to hear sounds at safe levels but reduce louder, harmful noises. Others have various kinds of acoustic baffles. Many promise improved comfort. Newer earmuff-style protectors come with electronics to help minimize the plugged-up and isolated feeling you can get from conventional muffs. Some have a microphone that picks up nearby sounds. Others have an FM/AM radio. Still others combine the microphone and the radio. What all these smart muffs have in common is the ability to cap the noise level hitting your ears at 80 to 82 db.

Noise-canceling headphones may be the most sophisticated type of hearing protector, but they may not be the best for woodworkers. Sold mainly to travelers seeking relief from the drone of jet engines, these headphones generate an inverted version of the

Noise levels, tool by tool

Sound is measured in decibels, a unit named for Alexander Graham Bell, who was known for his research into acoustics and deafness before he invented the telephone. The decibel scale is logarithmic, not linear. Every 3-db. increase means a doubling of the sound energy hitting the ear.

We can safely tolerate sounds up to about 85 db. But as the graph below shows, many shop machines emit much more sound. Past that 85-db. threshold, you must limit exposure and don hearing protectors to avoid long-term damage.

The National Institute for Occupational Safety and Health maintains an online database that lists the loudness of 120 popular tools from 14 manufacturers (www.cdc.gov/niosh-sound-vibration/). You also can play a 5-second-long audio file for each tool.

HEARING PROTECTORS NEEDED
FOR 8-HOUR EXPOSURE

2-HOUR
EXPOSURE

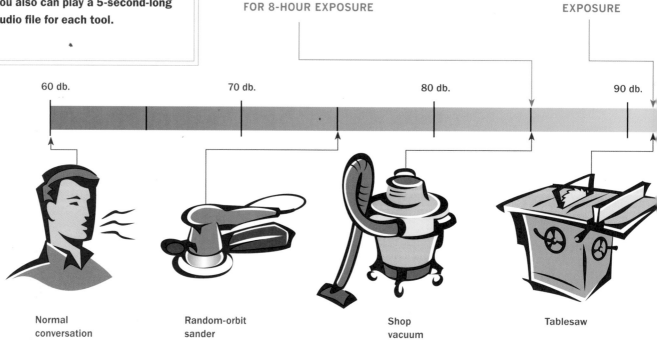

| 60 db. | 70 db. | 80 db. | 90 db. |

Normal conversation

Random-orbit sander

Shop vacuum

Tablesaw

Source: NIOSH data, author measurements

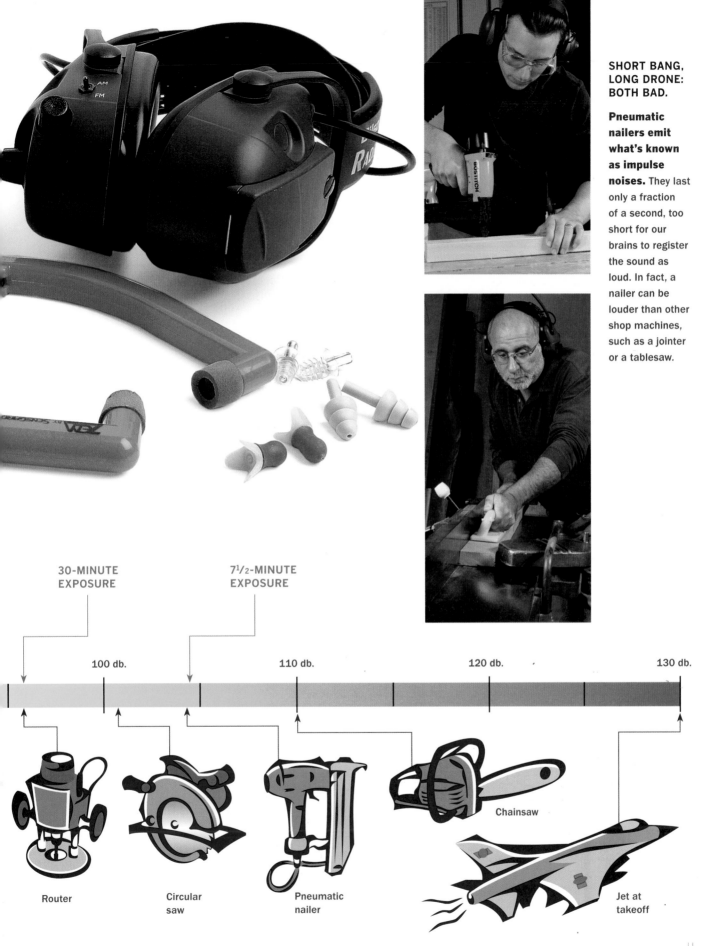

SHORT BANG, LONG DRONE: BOTH BAD.

Pneumatic nailers emit what's known as impulse noises. They last only a fraction of a second, too short for our brains to register the sound as loud. In fact, a nailer can be louder than other shop machines, such as a jointer or a tablesaw.

30-MINUTE EXPOSURE

7½-MINUTE EXPOSURE

100 db.

110 db.

120 db.

130 db.

Router

Circular saw

Pneumatic nailer

Chainsaw

Jet at takeoff

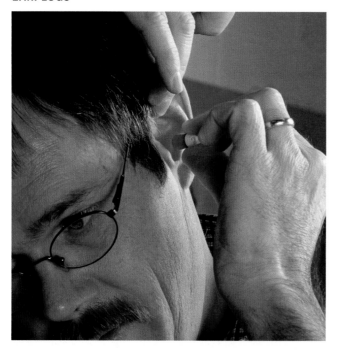

Simple and inexpensive, plugs can provide ample hearing protection. The ones shown here typify new designs that let normal sounds through but block harmful ones. The plug's biggest drawback is difficulty of use. Most are tricky to insert in the ear properly.

sound wave coming toward your ear, which effectively cancels the sound. Some researchers said that noise-canceling headphones work best with steady, constant sounds but are less effective with the relatively short bursts from shop machines.

All plugs and muffs can do the job...

Any hearing protector on the market will cut sound by 10 db. or more. Some claim to reduce sound by 25 db. or more. They're more than adequate for muffling the noise from machines in a home woodshop. In fact, it's pointless to try to figure out which specific hearing protector might actually offer a higher level of protection. Turns out, there's no way to know for sure.

BLAST BUSTERS SHOOTER'S EAR PLUGS

What it does: Reduces ambient noise levels by about 75%, but limits impact noise to 80-85 db.
Panelists' comments: Easy to use if wearing eye protection.
Source: www.earplugstore.com

HOCKS NOISE BRAKERS

What it does: Reduces all sound approximately to the volume of normal speech. Designed so that escaping sound waves cancel dangerous noises.
Panelists' comments: Lets voices through.
Source: www.hocksproducts.com

QUIETEAR

What it does: Reduces sound volume by half, with additional protection above 85 db.
Panelists' comments: Couldn't get them to fit.
Source: www.heartech.co.il

ZEM BY SENSGARD

What it does: Uses specially designed headband to direct sounds away from ears; filters out the most damaging frequencies.
Panelists' comments: Picked up too much ambient noise ("I could hear myself chewing my own gum.") Hard to adjust.
Source: www.zemzone.com

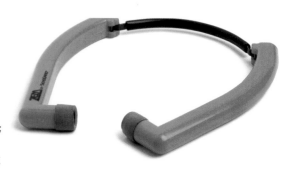

BILSOM ELECTO
What it does: Uses microphone to pick up ambient noise, and has built-in FM/AM radio. Sounds from mic or radio limited to 82 db.
Panelists' comments: Lightweight.
Source: www.earplugstore.com

BILSOM RADIO
What it does: Has built-in FM/AM radio. Radio's loudness limited to 82 db.
Panelists' comments: Good radio, but muffs not as comfortable as some others.
Source: www.earplugstore.com

ELVEX QUIETUNES COM-660
What it does: Has built-in FM/AM radio. Radio's loudness limited to 82-85 db.
Panelists' comments: Radio picked up static from shop machines.
Source: www.elvex.com

LEE VALLEY ELECTRONIC HEARING PROTECTORS
What it does: Uses microphone to pick up ambient noise. Sounds from mic limited to 85 db.
Panelists' comments: Liked ambient noise through microphone. Easy to use with eyeglasses.
Source: www.leevalley.com

MUFFS

Sophisticated new muffs, like those shown here, don't just cover your ears to block noise. Some contain electronics that let you hear some normal sounds but keep the noise at a safe level. Some offer built-in radios for entertainment and to reduce the sense of isolation.

Most hearing protectors carry a Noise Reduction Rating, or NRR. The number, derived from lab tests under ideal conditions, is supposed to indicate how many decibels of protection the product provides. But the lab tests don't track with real-world conditions. Each manufacturer does its own testing under somewhat different conditions, so the NRR can't be used to compare brands. It wasn't surprising that one government audiologist I spoke with joked that NRR actually means "not really relevant."

. . . so comfort and convenience are key

Hearing protectors range from disposable foam plugs that cost about a dollar a pair to electronics-laden earmuffs that sell for close to $200. What's best? Every expert I spoke with offered the same piece of advice: The best hearing protectors are the ones you'll wear regularly. That means you want something comfortable and easy to use.

To gauge the comfort and convenience of some new protectors, I asked several *Fine Woodworking* and *Fine Homebuilding* editors to make informal comparisons. Each person tried four hearing protectors—two earmuffs with built-in radios, microphones, or both and two sets of earplugs. I chose the products based on advice from experts and my own research.

People compared two products at a time, using noisy shop machines for 10-minute stretches. They had to decide whether they preferred one product, based on factors including ease of use, comfort, and whether the wearer still could hear normal sounds. I also asked if they would use the product regularly.

The panelists' favorites

Overall, people preferred earmuffs to plugs. It's simply easier to pop a set of muffs over your ears than to insert plugs every few minutes.

Most of the negative comments about earplugs concerned difficulty with fitting them into the ear. These plugs are only slightly easier to fit than older foam plugs. Yet nearly everyone said they liked a favorite plug or muff well enough to use it regularly.

Our favorite muffs were The Bilsom Radio, the Bilsom Electo (pricey muffs with both microphone and radio), and microphone-enhanced muffs from Lee Valley Tools. The Elvex® QuieTunes were least preferred; several people complained that the radio picked up static from shop machines.

Among earplugs, people said the Hocks Noise Brakers® allowed them to hear normal conversation. At least one person favored the QuietEar and BlastBuster™ plugs; others called them hard to put on. One tester preferred the unique Zem by Sensgard, designed to direct sounds away from the ear.

A Look at Eye Protection

STEVE SCOTT

As beautiful as it might look to you, a woodshop is an unfriendly environment for your eyes. Sanders kick up clouds of irritating dust. The tablesaw throws sharp chips, while small workpieces can burst into flying shards at the miter saw. The lathe peppers its user with wood chips, and grinders throw sparks and abrasive fragments. Handwork also presents dangers: A chisel and mallet can launch chips like little missiles. Less likely perhaps, but just as dangerous, is a caustic splash from a jostled container of solvent or finish.

According to government estimates, hospitals in 2004 treated about 15,000 eye injuries from tools found in most woodshops. Many of these injuries could have been avoided if the victim had worn an inexpensive set of safety glasses or goggles.

"These are not high-ticket items, compared to saving your sight," said Dr. Larry Jackson, an epidemiologist who studies workplace injuries at the National Institute for Occupational Safety and Health.

Jackson, who helped develop U.S. industry standards for safety glasses, recommends that every woodshop be equipped with all three basic types of safety eyewear—glasses, goggles,

Three lines of defense. Safety experts say there's a need in every woodshop for each of these forms of eye protection: safety glasses for jobs that shoot lightweight chips into the air, goggles to keep heavy dust out of your eyes, and face shields (used with glasses or goggles) to protect your face and repel heavier chips or other projectiles.

Safety glasses ward off small chips and dust. With impact-resistant lenses and frames and wraparound protection, safety glasses shield your eyes from small flying chips, whether they're launched by a mallet and chisel or by a powerful shop machine. There also are great options for woodworkers with corrected vision.

Good protection isn't costly. The inexpensive Elvex Triad offers no-nonsense eye protection in sporty wraparound frames. The glasses feature a flexible nose bridge and earpieces for added comfort.

The Cadillac. The ESS® ICE 2.4™ offers military level impact resistance and greater visibility. The frameless design doesn't interfere with peripheral vision, a common complaint about some protective eyewear. The military cachet comes at a price, though.

and face shields. Woodworkers should use some type of eye protection at all times in the shop, he says.

No doubt some woodworkers will balk at that suggestion—it's hard to believe that your eyesight is threatened when you're taking shavings with a block plane or laying out dovetails with a marking gauge and a bevel. But it's also hard to argue against a sure way of keeping your eyes safe: making a rigorous habit of wearing the right protective gear. The argument tilts further when you consider how easy it is to find comfortable and effective eye protection.

Every woodworker will strike his or her own balance between convenience and eye safety. Three *Fine Woodworking* editors sized up a broad selection of glasses and goggles, looking for models that offer both protection and comfort. Here's an informal overview of the eyewear that's available with some tips on what to look for.

Safety glasses are a must

Any protective eyewear—glasses or goggles—should meet the American National Safety Institute standard known as Z87.1-2003. This means that the lenses, typically made of tough polycarbonate, won't shatter and the frames won't break when smacked by a ¼-in. BB moving at 150 ft. per second. They must also offer generous side protection to keep dust and flying objects out of the corners of your eyes. The lenses, frames, and packaging should all be stamped with a Z87+ to indicate that they meet this safety standard.

Don't wear glasses?—For the woodworker who doesn't wear glasses or who wears contact lenses, the selection of safety glasses is wide and varied. Most fit and look like lightweight sport sunglasses.

We liked lightweight models from Elvex and Edge Eyewear that had large, wraparound lenses for good peripheral vision. UVEX, Crews, and AO Safety also make suitable and inexpensive models.

To aid in a snug and comfortable fit, some models come with a padded or flexible nose bridge, padding at the browline, and adjustable earpieces.

Plenty of options for glasses wearers—If you wear glasses, you might think they give you adequate eye protection in the shop. They don't.

Your glasses very likely offer no side protection at all, and they probably leave too much room between your brow or cheekbones and the rims of the glasses. Wood-chip projectiles can dart through that gap. Some street glasses also have lenses of glass or acrylic that might not stand up to a direct hit from flying debris.

Safety glasses go a long way toward correcting these flaws. They are designed to fit closely to your brow and cheekbones, and they feature wraparound lenses or side shields

Prescription safety glasses can be stylish. Optometrists, vision centers, and online retailers offer plenty of styles for safety frames and prescription lenses that meet industry standards for impact protection. This pair is from Phillips Safety Products.

Glasses for your glasses. Safety eyewear designed to fit over street glasses is a relatively inexpensive way for prescription wearers to protect their eyes in the shop. This pair from Eye Armor offers a snug fit.

to protect the corners of your eyes. The lenses and the frames both are impact resistant.

There are plenty of safety glasses designed to fit over the glasses you already wear. They are sturdy and inexpensive, but the challenge lies in getting a good fit.

Low profile. For folks who don't wear prescription lenses, many goggles offer a streamlined profile. Uvex Spoggles are one example.

Roomy enough to fit over glasses. It's easy to find goggles that fit comfortably over your street glasses. Verdict Goggles by Crews offer indirect air baffles for fog control and splash protection.

Convertible models. Some glasses or goggles can be fitted with inserts that hold prescription optics. Others, like the SG1 from Wiley X™, can be fitted directly with prescription lenses.

Goggles seal out dust. They offer the same impact protection as safety glasses, but safety goggles close all the gaps between your face and the lens with a foam or rubber lining. This full protection is needed when you're filling the air with clouds of fine dust.

Safety frames for prescription lenses range from bland and square to sleek and stylish. There are a few wraparound models, but lenses of this shape cannot be ground to fit some prescriptions.

If you wear contacts, you still need safety glasses or goggles to keep your eyes safe. Some safety experts go further and advise against wearing contacts in environments with a lot of dust or chemical fumes in the air because either of these could become trapped behind the lens and damage your eye. Hard lenses are more likely to trap dust; soft lenses are more vulnerable to chemicals, the experts say. Injury statistics typically don't track contact-lens use, so it's hard to gauge the threat. The safest course may be to always use goggles over contacts or to take the contacts out and wear glasses instead when you're in the shop.

Jackson and others recommend wearing safety glasses for any light-duty shop activity that doesn't involve power tools. For power tools that throw dust and chips at high speed, they recommend stepping up to goggles.

Face shields protect head and neck. A face shield is essential at the lathe, which can spray its user with heavy chips. Flying sparks or disintegrating grinder wheels also are a threat. Be sure to wear safety glasses or goggles underneath; flying debris can ricochet behind the mask.

Goggles provide more comprehensive coverage

Goggles are the most certain way of protecting your eyes from fast-flying debris and heavy floating dust. They're better at this than safety glasses because they completely enclose the eyes, and they're held snug to your face with an elastic head strap. Models with baffled air vents provide the best dust protection and also can protect your eyes against chemical splashes.

For the best field of view, we preferred the full-face models that resemble a diver's mask to the motorcyclist style with separate eyepieces.

Some models, like the goggles you wore in high school chemistry lab, are designed to fit over glasses. Those very goggles, in fact, or ones much like them, are a great and inexpensive way to protect your eyes in the shop. But with their rubbery, scuba-mask feel, you might not want to wear them for long. A roomy, updated version from Crews has baffled air vents and a foam lining. It's more comfortable but still bulky.

Updated version of the basic shield. Jackson and Uvex offer two slightly different takes on the familiar face-shield design. Jackson's The Shield mates a set of safety goggles with an impact-resistant shield for the lower face. The Bionic Face Shield by Uvex provides extended coverage for the chin and the top of the head.

When the heavy chips fly, reach for a face shield

Any task in which the tool forcefully throws large wood chips or other heavy flying particles (wood turning, for instance) calls for a face shield.

A face shield consists of a large, clear visor mounted on a piece of adjustable headgear to flip up and down like a welder's mask. Inexpensive models are available from both Woodcraft and Lee Valley Tools. Just like its name implies, a face shield is designed to prevent flying objects from striking the wearer in the face.

It's easy to feel like your eyes are well protected behind this clear shell, but safety experts say otherwise. Because a face shield is more or less open at the bottom, wood chips or other projectiles could get past it and into your eye. For that reason, the experts say, you should always wear safety glasses or goggles under a face shield. A face shield for your face, glasses or goggles for your eyes.

Metric Equivalents

INCHES	CENTIMETERS	MILLIMETERS	INCHES	CENTIMETERS	MILLIMETERS
⅛	0.3	3	13	33.0	330
¼	0.6	6	14	35.6	356
⅜	1.0	10	15	38.1	381
½	1.3	13	16	40.6	406
⅝	1.6	16	17	43.2	432
¾	1.9	19	18	45.7	457
⅞	2.2	22	19	48.3	483
1	2.5	25	20	50.8	508
1¼	3.2	32	21	53.3	533
1½	3.8	38	22	55.9	559
1¾	4.4	44	23	58.4	584
2	5.1	51	24	61	610
2½	6.4	64	25	63.5	635
3	7.6	76	26	66.0	660
3½	8.9	89	27	68.6	686
4	10.2	102	28	71.7	717
4½	11.4	114	29	73.7	737
5	12.7	127	30	76.2	762
6	15.2	152	31	78.7	787
7	17.8	178	32	81.3	813
8	20.3	203	33	83.8	838
9	22.9	229	34	86.4	864
10	25.4	254	35	88.9	889
11	27.9	279	36	91.4	914
12	30.5	305			

Contributors

Andy Beasley lives in Colorado Springs, CO.

Asa Christiana is the editor of *Fine Woodworking*.

Scott Gibson, a contributing writer to *Fine Homebuilding*, lives in Maine.

Chris Gochnour, the owner of the Joiners Bench in Murray, UT , has been building fine furniture for the past 20 years. He teaches furniture making at Salt Lake Community College, the Traditional Building Skill Institute at Snow College, and the Marc Adams School of Woodworking. Visit him online at www. chrisgochnour.com.

Garrett Hack, a professional furniture maker and woodworking instructor, is a contributing editor to *Fine Woodworking*.

David Heim is a former associate editor at *Fine Woodworking*. He now divides his time between freelance editing, woodturning, and SketchUp artistry at his home in Oxford, CT.

Nancy McCoy is a certified lighting designer in Novato, CA. Her husband, **Peter Judge**, is an avid woodworker.

Thomas McKenna is *Fine Woodworking's* managing editor.

Jeff Miller is a furniture designer, craftsman, teacher, and author of woodworking books and a frequent contributor to *Fine Woodworking* and other publications. Jeff's furniture has been shown in galleries and shows nationwide and has won numerous awards. His furniture is in the Decorative Arts Collection of the Chicago History Museum. Visit him online at www. furnituremaking.com.

Bill Peck is shop manager for *Fine Woodworking*.

Michael Pekovich is *Fine Woodworking's* art director.

Clifford A. Popejoy is a licensed electrical contractor and occasional woodworker in Sacramento, CA.

Michael Puryear is a designer/furnituremaker practicing his craft in the Catskills of New York. Visit him online at www.michaelpuryear.com.

Bruce Ryden is a retired fire-safety inspector.

Steve Scott is a *Fine Woodworking* associate editor.

Stelios L.A. Stavrinides AKA Steliart is a graphic Web designer and woodworker in Nicosia, Cyprus.

Patrick Sullivan is an internal medicine specialist with extensive emergency room experience. Now retired from his medical practice, he has more time for woodworking.

Matthew Teague builds furniture in Nashville, TN, and is the editor of *Popular Woodworking Magazine*.

John White, an experienced designer, cabinetmaker, and machinist, managed the *Fine Woodworking* woodshop for almost a decade. Now he splits his time between writing, teaching, designing, and consulting from his home in Rochester, VT. You can reach him by email at zensmithvt@gmail.com.

Credits

All photos are courtesy of *Fine Woodworking* magazine © The Taunton Press, Inc., except as noted below:

Front cover: Main photo by Patrick McCombe, left photos top to bottom: Michael Pekovich and Tom Begnal. Back cover from top to bottom: Thomas McKenna, Matt Kenney, and John Tetreault.

The articles in this book appeared in the following issues of *Fine Woodworking*:

pp. 4-12: 15 Tips for Basement Workshops by Thomas McKenna, issue 202. Photos by staff except for photos p. 7 and p. 12 by Robert Beason, top photo p. 8 by Art Mulder, bottom photo p. 8, top photo p. 9, and top photo p. 11 by Dave Verstraete, middle photo p. 8 and bottom photo p. 11 by Serge Duclos, and photo p. 10 by Christopher Walvoord. Drawing pp. 4-5 by John Hartman and drawing p. 7 by Vince Babak.

pp. 13-24: Turn Your Garage Into a Real Workshop by Michael Pekovich, issue 216. Photos by Rachel Barclay except photos p. 13 and p. 18 by Patrick McCombe. Drawings by John Hartman.

pp. 25-37: Smart Garage Workshop, From the Ground Up by Matthew Teague, issue 195. Photos by Asa Christiana except for photo p. 28 and all photos pp. 26-27 by Matthew Teague except bottom photo p. 27 by James Lennon. Drawings by Toby Welles @ Design Core.

pp. 38-43: Shop Design: Think Your Shop is Small? Think Again by Stelios L.A. Stavrinides, issue 216. Photos by Stelios Athrakiotis. SketchUp drawings by author; final renderings by Dave Richards.

pp. 44-51: Wiring a Workshop by Clifford A. Popejoy, issue 188. Photos by Kelly J. Dunton except for top photo p. 47 by Rodney Diaz, center photo p. 47 by Mark Schofield, and bottom photo p. 47 by Tom Begnal. Drawings by Brian Jensen.

pp. 52-61: Let There Be Light by Nancy McCoy and Peter Judge, issue 209. Photos by Michael Pekovich except for photos pp. 58-59 by Kelly J. Dunton. Drawings by Michael Pekovich.

pp. 62-67: Treat Your Feet by Steve Scott, issue 216. Photos by Kelly J. Dunton. Drawing by *Fine Woodworking* staff.

pp. 68-73: Low-Cost Shop Floor by Scott Gibson, issue 160. Photos by Tim Sams. Drawings by Vince Babak.

pp. 74-85: A Revolution in Dust Collection by Asa Christiana, issue 223. Photos by Michael Pekovich. Drawings by Stephen Hutchings.

pp. 86-97: A Workbench 30 Years in the Making by Garrett Hack, issue 209. Photos by Thomas McKenna. Drawings by David Richards.

pp. 98-109: The Wired Workbench by John White, issue 223. Photos by Matt Kenney. Drawings by John Hartman.

pp. 110-115: Making Sense of Vises by Garrett Hack, issue 191. Photos by Steve Scott. Drawings by John Hartman.

pp. 116-124: Your Miter Saw Needs a Stand by John White, issue 209. Photos by *Fine Woodworking* staff. Drawings by Jim Richey.

pp. 125-136: Best-Ever Outfeed Table by John White, issue 202. Photos by Matt Kenney except for photos p. 126 by John Tetreault. Drawings by Bob La Pointe.

pp. 137-145: Pivoting Plywood Cart by Michael Puryear, issue 223. Photos by Anissa Kapsales. Drawings by Jim Richey.

pp. 146-157: House Your Tools in High Style by Chris Gochnour, issue 223. Photos by Thomas McKenna. Drawings by Bob La Pointe.

pp. 158-163: Keep Planes Close at Hand by Chris Gochnour, issue 209. Photos by Thomas McKenna. Drawings by Bob La Pointe.

pp. 164-167: Divide and Conquer by Michael Pekovich, issue 223. Photos by Steve Scott.

pp. 168-173: Lumber Storage Solutions by Andy Beasley, issue 181. Photos by Tom Begnal. Drawings by Jim Richey.

pp. 174-181: Fire Safety in the Shop by Bruce Ryden, issue 174. Photos by William Duckworth except for photo p. 175 by John Hamel courtesy of Ellis Wallentine and photos p. 176, middle photo p. 178, and top and bottom photos p. 179 by Rodney Diaz. Drawing by Vince Babak.

pp. 182-193: Cutting-Edge First Aid by Patrick Sullivan, issue 216. Photos by John Tetreault. Drawings by Christopher Mills.

pp. 194-200: Protect Yourself from Wood Dust by Jeff Miller, issue 201. Photos by Matt Kenney. Drawings by John Tetreault.

pp. 201-206: Sound Advice by David Heim, issue 189. Photos by David Heim except for top photo pp. 202-203 by Kelly J. Dunton. Drawings by Stephen Hutchings.

pp. 207-212: A New Look at Eye Protection by Steve Scott, issue 187. Photos by Rodney Diaz except for the product shots by Kelly J. Dunton.

Index